Advocacy in Counseling

Counselors, Clients, & Community

Edited by
Judy Lewis and Loretta J. Bradley

In association with the ERIC Counseling
and Student Services Clearinghouse

ISBN 1-56109-087-5

This publication was funded in part by the US
Department of Education, Office of Educational
Research and Improvement, Contract no. ED-99-CO-
0014.Opinions expressed in this publication do not
necessarily reflect the positions of the US Department
of Education, OERI, or ERIC/CASS.

In association with the ERIC Counseling
and Student Services Clearinghouse

ISBN 56109-08-5

This publication was funded in part by the
Department of Education, Office of Educational
Research and Improvement, Contract No. ED-
99-CO-0014. Opinions in this publication do not
necessarily reflect the positions of the U.S. Department
of Education, OERI, or ERIC/CASS.

Table of Contents

Foreword

This is an excellent book for any contemporary counselor. Advocacy is an essential role which counselors must perform, be it a matter of speaking out or working to make changes in the environment. However, being an advocate requires more than desire on the part of the counselor. It requires knowhow! Unfortunately, knowhow as regards client or political advocacy is not commonly practiced by counselors.

This book which identifies 15 specific advocacy issues and/or populations directly responds to the need for counselor knowhow about advocacy. It has been sorely needed.

Loretta Bradley and Judy Lewis are to be commended for undertaking the development of this publication. Richard Yep and the American Counseling Foundation are also deserving of appreciation for their active support of the project culminating in this publication. The authors are also to be commended for producing pithy and highly worthwhile papers.

From the initial conception of the project I have been an enthusiastic supporter. We are pleased to be able to convert the excellent papers which first appeared in *Counseling Today* into a full fledged publication. This book follows an outstanding publication by ERIC/CASS and ACA on advocacy by Courtland Lee—*Social Action: A Mandate for Counselors*. Also the excellent publication by ERIC/CASS, *Cultural and Diversity Issues in Counseling*, authored by Paul B. Pedersen and Don C. Locke, is a very useful publication on counseling advocacy by identifying the needs of different population groups.

These publications arm a counselor to undertake effective advocacy. We believe you will find them to be highly useful resources!

Garry R. Walz, Ph.D., NCC
Director, ERIC/CASS

Preface

As the Executive Director of the American Counseling Association, I have regarded assisting the elected leadership to implement their goals for the Association as a major priority. I therefore have worked closely with Loretta Bradley on developing her presidential theme of Advocacy. It is a very timely theme which is of the utmost importance for ACA and its membership. I was most pleased to work with her to further her presidential theme both as the ACA Executive Director and in my role as Secretary of the ACA Foundation. The appointment of Judy Lewis to head the writing team and to have the papers published in *Counseling Today* were steps I also strongly supported.

I was also gratified to work with Garry Walz, Director of ERIC/CASS to see the project through to the publication of this monograph by ERIC/CASS. The papers are well written and in conjunction with the ERIC searches offered in the publication provide a very useful resource for counselors. I do hope you act on the ideas presented in this monograph, as it will benefit you and the Association.

Richard Yep
Executive Director
American Counseling Association

Advocacy in Counseling

Edited by
Judy Lewis and Loretta J. Bradley

Advocacy is an important aspect of every counselor's role. Regardless of the particular setting in which he or she works, each counselor is confronted again and again with issues that cannot be resolved simply through change within the individual. All too often, negative aspects of the environment impinge on a client's well-being, intensifying personal problems or creating obstacles to growth. When such situations arise, effective counselors speak up!

We think of advocacy as the act of speaking up or taking action to make environmental changes on behalf of our clients. Sometimes, these actions take the form of *client advocacy* and are directed toward making the environment more responsive to the needs of an individual. Just as often, counselors find that they need to focus their actions on *political advocacy*, influencing political, economic and social systems that oppress a whole population of clients. The chapters that follow all show how these ideas can be operationalized in practice.

The chapters in this volume have been selected from among "advocacy theme papers" that were written by members of the American Counseling Association during Loretta J. Bradley's term as president of the association. Bradley selected as her presidential theme *Advocacy: A Voice for Our Clients and Communities*. In keeping with this theme, Bradley asked Judy Lewis to edit a set of invited papers related to advocacy. An Advocacy Theme Task Force, chaired by Lewis and composed of Stuart Chen-Hayes, Doris Rhea Coy, Mark S. Kiselcia, Jo-Ann Lipford Sanders, and Derald Wing Sue, acted as editorial board, generating topics, identifying authors, and reviewing papers. Each author was asked to do the following:

- Address a specific issue or population.
- Provide a rationale for using advocacy as an approach for dealing with the issue or meeting the needs of the population.
- Suggest strategies for client and political advocacy.
- Suggest resources for additional study.

As the chapters that follow indicate, all of the issues addressed lent themselves very clearly to advocacy strategies. Just as apparent is the topics. Whatever school or community is being served, whatever clients are being counseled, members of the counseling profession will find opportunities to work as advocates.

We are gratified that the counseling profession has moved so readily to embrace advocacy strategies. We particularly would like to thank the people who played important roles in bringing the advocacy theme papers to the attention of counselors and other helping professionals. These people include the American Counseling Association Foundation, which supported the production of the original papers; Richard Yep and the other members of the ACA staff who worked on production and dissemination; Garry Walz, who was enthusiastic about this project from the beginning and who has made this step in dissemination possible; the members of the Advocacy Theme Task Force; the authors of the papers; and the clients and communities that have inspired us.

Judy Lewis
Loretta Bradley

Editor's note: This series of advocacy papers is being published in concert with the American Counseling Association President Loretta Bradley's year-long theme. The papers have been selected by the Task Force on Advocacy: Judith A. Lewis (chair), Stuart Chen-Hayes, Doris Rhea Coy, Mark S. Kiselica, Jo-Ann Lipford Sanders, and Derald Wing Sue. Production has been underwritten by the ACA Foundation. All advocacy papers are available on ACA's website at **www.counseling.org**.

ERIC/CASS assumed responsibility for printing and marketing the publication. All papers will be availale in full text in the ERIC database. For full details, call ERIC/CASS at 800-414-9769

Developing a Common Language and Framework for Understanding Advocacy in Counseling

Rebecca L. Toporek

Recently, there has been a resurgence of literature around the topic of advocacy in counseling. An increasing amount of theory and research suggests that the field of counseling must seriously consider the role of advocacy in counseling practice (Atkinson, Thompson, & Grant, 1993; Enns, 1993; Esquivel & Keitel, 1990; Grevious, 1985; Sodowsky, Kuo-Jackson, & Loya, 1996). The 1999 Presidential Theme for the American Counseling Association (ACA) is bringing advocacy to the forefront and focusing concentrated efforts on advocacy in practice and training in the field. The purpose of this paper is to present a framework and definitions that may be useful in considering the role of advocacy in counseling. Using this framework as a foundation, I will review advocacy in counseling and discuss examples of a range of advocacy actions. In addition, I will propose some of the possible reasons why advocacy has historically experienced marginalization in counseling. My ultimate intention is to facilitate counselors in identifying the range of appropriate ways that they may advocate for clients and client groups.

Historically, the focus of counseling has been to facilitate clients toward adapting to the environment. However, advocacy in counseling asserts that the environment must change and that both the counselor and client may be instrumental in this change. While little attention has been given to the role of advocacy in counseling, some supporting literature has come from community counseling, multicultural counseling, and feminist therapy. Within the larger profession, there have been some organizational efforts to address advocacy. However, there has been a lack of training and agreement about philosophy, definitions, and methods of implementation. Thus, the term "advocacy" appears to refer to a wide range of activities in which counselors and counseling psychologists may engage. In addition, there is a lack of consistency in the endorsement of the advocate role as being appropriate in counseling. It is important to examine these contradictions in order to adequately address and conceptualize the future of advocacy in the counseling profession.

In this paper, I am choosing to focus on advocacy that has, as its intent, a direct focus on clients and client groups. The activities of professional organizations often identify advocacy in terms of advocacy for the profession. In other words, many efforts have emphasized professional involvement in legislation regarding the counseling profession, licensing boards, and managed care systems as a way of maintaining the competitiveness of the field with other helping professions. This type of advocacy has gone largely unchallenged in the counseling profession. While this form of advocacy may benefit clients indirectly, it is only one form of advocacy and is often seen as self-serving. In the remainder of this paper and the model I present, advocacy will not include these types of efforts.

In this paper, I will define advocacy as "action taken by a counseling professional to facilitate the removal of external and institutional barriers to clients' well-being" (Toporek & Liu, in press). In this definition, experiences with clients and specific client issues are the focus of the counselor's advocacy actions and goals. Two other issues are also important. First, there is an assumption that counselors are in positions of institutional power and privilege in relation to clients. This asserts that counselors have access to resources and policies in a way that is different from those available to clients. Advocacy recognizes that the professional position of the counselor, their institutional involvement, and the ascribed credibility of their role and stature, may influence policy and practice in a way that is unavailable to many clients. The second issue of importance is that this definition does not assume that clients are unable to advocate for themselves. Rather, there are certain groups of clients who are the recipients of institutionalized oppression in this country. Specifically, oppression due to race, class, gender, sexual orientation, and physical ability has historically determined the institutional power accessible to many clients and client groups. While many counselors may also be members of these groups, they still hold a certain access to the profession and policy making at a level often unattainable to clients. In reality, the majority of counselors belong to dominant groups and have been the recipients of less oppression. For example, the great majority of counselors are White, well-educated, middle class, heterosexual, and lack significant physical disabilities. A great number of counselors are White women and therefore face some gender bias in society. However, they are recipients of privilege due to their socioracial identity in society and within the profession they have influence due to their majority.

A Framework for Understanding Advocacy

The working definition of "advocacy" in this paper reflects some concepts presented by Lewis et al. (1998). They suggested that advocacy "serves two primary purposes: (1) increasing clients' sense of personal power and (2) fostering environmental changes that reflect greater responsiveness to their personal needs" (p. 172).

Given the definition of advocacy used in this paper, and the assertions of Lewis et al. (1998), a model of advocacy may be seen as a continuum encompassing empowerment and social action (Toporek & Liu, in press). In this model, advocacy serves as an umbrella concept with empowerment on one end of a continuum and social action on the other. This continuum summarizes a range of activities in which counselors may advocate for clients and client issues. An awareness of sociopolitical forces exists throughout the continuum. However, the context within which the counselor takes action varies along this continuum. Counselor actions that tend to focus within the individual or group counseling environment and assist clients in recognizing and addressing sociopolitical barriers to well-being would lie toward the empowerment end of the continuum. Whereas, counselor actions that advocate for change in the context of a large, public arena would lie toward the social action end of the continuum. I will provide some examples from counseling literature to illustrate what this might look like in counseling. But first, it is important to establish some working definitions of empowerment and social action.

The definition of empowerment in this model "embodies the interpersonal interactions between the therapist and client working within the socioeconomic, sociocultural and sociopolitical context" (Toporek & Liu, in press). Often, in more traditional definitions of empowerment, the focus of counseling is to facilitate the client's sense of self-efficacy during counseling. On the surface, this accurately reflects one aspect of our definition of empowerment. However, traditional definitions typically have avoided references to sociopolitical variables affecting barriers to client action. In addition, the focus on empowerment in traditional, intrapsychically focused counseling does not suggest counselor involvement in the client's external environment. In fact, involvement in clients' external environments tends to be discouraged and considered a risk for disempowering clients or creating the potential for dual roles. In contrast, McWhirter (1994) emphasized that empowerment must take into account the sociopolitical context within which our clients live. To ignore this aspect is to ignore a crucial influence in empowerment. In the advocacy continuum client goals are placed at the forefront. In empowerment forms of advocacy, the means of achieving these goals may include a counselor's initial involvement in the client's environment while the client moves toward acting independently to challenge their environment. For example, a counselor may help a client to recognize an external barrier that is influencing their well-being and strategize ways of confronting it. The counselor may decide to initially accompany the client in approaching the source of their difficulty (e.g., a hostile teacher).

The other end of the advocacy continuum reflects social action. Social action refers to counselors' participation in the larger sociopolitical context to facilitate the removal of barriers faced by his/her clients or client groups. Thus, social action may include advocacy in a large, public arena. For example, a counselor may become actively involved in legislative or policy issues directly affecting clients and client issues. This type of action reflects the concept of "class advocacy" identified by Lewis et al. (1998). This is in contrast to advocacy around a specific situation or issue faced by a particular client.

Supportive Literature in Advocacy, Empowerment and Social Action

There are several areas of counseling that have provided consistent support for advocacy in counseling. For example, multicultural counseling, feminist therapy, and community counseling have maintained that advocacy is an important and integral role in counseling. This literature provides some specific examples of how advocacy, empowerment and social action may be implemented in counseling.

In multicultural counseling, some authors have suggested that it is necessary to expand traditional counseling professional roles to include advocacy (Atkinson et al., 1993; Esquivel & Keitel, 1990). Leung (1995) suggested that counselors should be active in systemically changing environments (i.e., reduction of barriers for clients of color) in order to facilitate better educational and career development. Hotchkiss and Borow (1990) provided examples of empowerment and advocacy in career counseling by suggesting that the counseling role may include helping clients to complete job applications and to strategize about dealing with discrimination. Arredondo et al. (1996) presented an example of an advocacy opportunity for counselors within higher education. In their example, a counselor received numerous complaints from students of color about a particular faculty member. The counselor may facilitate students' understanding of the discrimination complaint process (empowerment) and then go a step beyond by intervening at an institutional policy level (social action).

In feminist therapy and counseling, there has traditionally been a focus on client advocacy, empowerment, and social action (Enns, 1993). From this perspective, empowerment in counseling has included encouraging clients' awareness of the sociopolitical forces that impinge on their mental health. In addition, there is a focus on facilitating action to change these systems. As an example of this approach, Comas-Díaz (1987) suggested an empowerment model of therapy. This model may help Latina clients to understand the effects of racism and sexism, work with the feelings resulting from degradation inherent in the status imposed upon them in society, recognize their role as agents in the solutions to their problems, see the interplay between external forces and their internal difficulties, and identify opportunities for making changes in the larger society.

In community counseling, Lewis and Lewis (1983) and Lewis et al. (1998) presented detailed discussions of various forms of advocacy. One of the examples provided by Lewis et al. (1998) suggested an advocacy situation in which a single teenage parent was denied public education. They suggested an expansion of the counselor's role to directly confront the system with the intention to change policy and support the client's right to an education.

Recently, more literature on social action in counseling has become available. *Social action: A Mandate for Counselors* (Lee & Walz, 1998) provides chapters by various authors addressing multiple forms of social action and its role in counseling. Many counselors may find this to be an invaluable resource.

Social action may take many forms ranging from local institutional change to influencing public policy and federal legislation. Individual counselors have pursued social action and advocacy in terms of legislative and policy issues as well as through professional associations. Advocacy within professional associations can ultimately contribute to clients' well-being in two ways. First, advocacy may work toward minimizing institutional barriers within the profession. Second, advocacy actions can include enhancing our ability to provide service to individuals and groups who have traditionally been oppressed. The efforts to establish standards of multicultural counseling competence within ACA (Sue, Arredondo & McDavis, 1992) represent one example of this type of advocacy. Many individuals within ACA have worked toward facilitating the adoption of these competencies into accreditation and standards of ethics (Arredondo et al., 1996; D'Andrea & Daniels, 1995; Sue et al., 1992). This type of advocacy directly affects clients who have been traditionally underserved or inappropriately counseled in the past due to neglect of the needs of individuals from diverse racial and ethnic backgrounds.

Other individuals have worked to bring advocacy and social action to the forefront of the profession. Several professional counseling associations have integrated some form of advocacy into their identity. Some of the most notable actions within ACA have been the 1998 Presidential Theme of Social Action and the 1999 Presidential Theme of Advocacy. While the efforts of the ACA Presidential Themes may help encourage advocacy in counseling, there continues to be disagreement about the appropriateness of direct client advocacy. In addition, there has been considerable debate about how "political" these organizations should be in terms of their advocacy.

Advocacy as social action may also be seen in the involvement of individuals in ACA to facilitate position statements that affect federal legislation. This form of advocacy attempts to influence the treatment and experience of large groups of individuals and client populations (e.g., clients of color, gay, lesbian, and bisexual clients). This form of advocacy has been consistently challenged within professional organizations. For example, statements were approved last year by the ACA Human Rights Committee regarding nonsupport for conversion therapy and the denouncement of brutality against gay, lesbian, and bisexual individuals in China. A number of members and divisions of ACA vigorously contested these Committee actions. Similarly, the Public Interest Directorate of the American Psychological Association (APA) has made several public statements supporting legislation affecting low income, immigration, education, and social issues (Tomes, April, 1997). They also have received considerable opposition by some individual members of APA.

Professional Issues Influencing the Implementation
of Advocacy Roles in Counseling

There are numerous unresolved issues that affect the implementation of advocacy roles in counseling. First, many counselors and counseling psychologists have disagreed about the degree to which "politics" should be involved in counseling. Some authors (e.g., Katz, 1985) asserted that traditional approaches to counseling have always been political because they have served to maintain the status quo. Other counseling professionals oppose social action advocacy on the grounds that counseling should be apolitical.

Another issue is the lack of training for appropriate advocacy in counseling. This is critical because there are ethical issues involved with advocacy as with all other aspects of counseling. There is a danger that some clients may perceive some advocacy actions when applied inappropriately, to be condescending and disempowering . Similarly, the counselor must be clear of his or her own intentions in advocacy work. For example, a White counselor who advocates to "help those people" or whose actions are motivated out of a sense of guilt, may perpetuate the power imbalance in the system as opposed to eliminating it. In addition, appropriate advocacy requires collaboration on the part of the counselor and client. Current issues around dual roles and other ethical issues set boundaries that need to be examined to allow for appropriate advocacy.

Another area of difficulty is that traditional values in counseling have emphasized intrapsychic approaches and internal locus of control. These represent particular cultural worldviews that de-emphasize sociopolitical and environmental issues in counseling. Cultural values such as independence, self-sufficiency, and personal responsibility have shaped the ways we have been trained to view client problems and provide interventions and treatment. Therefore, the type of theoretical framework and treatment approaches tend to be based on internal attributions of client problems and minimize the importance of addressing external barriers. Due to this focus in training, many counselors may lack the ability to recognize the role of external factors and the competence to address them through counseling interventions.

Finally, the settings within which counselors work may influence the implementation of advocacy. This may occur simply because the administration does not view advocacy as a valuable role or because the counselor's advocacy actions may actually challenge the policies and practices of the organization. As a result, there are limits on time and resources making advocacy actions more difficult.

Conclusion

Using a model of advocacy that includes a range of activities from empowerment to social action may be helpful in identifying action that may facilitate clients' well-being. Although the concept of advocacy in counseling is not entirely new, there are few guidelines and little training available to assist counselors in appropriately taking on this role. The 1999 ACA Presidential Theme marks a pivotal point in the history of counseling. This is one of the first comprehensive efforts to provide literature, examples, and guidance for counselors in a wide range of settings, with a diversity of clients, and through multiple and varied means. More specifically, the Advocacy Paper Series can serve as an invaluable resource for those counselors, counselor educators, and program developers beginning the implementation of advocacy or reinforcing current advocacy actions.

References

Arredondo, P., Toporek, R., Brown, S.P., Jones, J., Locke, D.C., Sanchez, J., & Stadler, H. (1996). Operationalization of the multicultural counseling competencies. *Journal of Multicultural Counseling & Development, 24*(1), 42-78.

Atkinson, D.R., Thompson, C.E., & Grant, S.K. (1993). A three-dimensional model for counseling racial/ethnic minorities. *The Counseling Psychologist, 21*(2), 257-277.

Comas-Díaz, L. (1987). Feminist therapy with mainland Puerto Rican women. *Psychology of Women Quarterly, 11*, 461-474.

D'Andrea, M., & Daniels, J. (1995). Promoting multiculturalism and organizational change in the counseling profession: A case study. In J.G. Ponterotto, J.M. Casas, L.A. Suzuki, & C.M. Alexander (Eds.), *Handbook of multicultural counseling* (pp. 17-33). Thousand Oaks, CA: Sage Publications, Inc.

Enns, C.Z. (1993). Twenty years of feminist counseling and therapy: From naming biases to implementing multifaceted practice. *The Counseling Psychologist, 21*(1), 3-87.

Esquivel, G.B., & Keitel, M.A. (1990). Counseling immigrant children in the schools. *Elementary School Guidance and Counseling, 24,* 213-221.

Grevious, C. (1985). The role of the family therapist with low-income Black families. *Family Therapy, 12*(2), 115-122.

Hotchkiss, L., & Borow, H. (1990). Sociological perspectives on work and career development. In D. Brown, L. Brooks, & Associates (Eds.), *Career choice and development* (2nd ed.) (pp. 262-307). San Francisco: Jossey-Bass.

Katz, J.H. (1985). The sociopolitical nature of counseling. *The Counseling Psychologist, 13*(4), 615-624.

McWhirter, E.H. (1994). *Counseling for empowerment.* Alexandria, VA: American Counseling Association.

Lee, C.C., & Walz, G.R. (Eds.). (1998). *Social action: A mandate for counselors,* Alexandria, VA: American Counseling Association.

Leung, S.A. (1995). Career development and counseling: A multicultural perspective. In J.G. Ponterotto, J.M. Casas, L.A. Suzuki, & C.M. Alexander (Eds.), *Handbook of multicultural counseling* (pp. 549-566). Thousand Oaks, CA: Sage Publications, Inc.

Lewis, J.A., & Lewis, M.D. (1983). *Community counseling: A human services approach* 2nd Ed., New York: John Wiley & Sons.

Lewis, J.A., Lewis, M.D., Daniels, J.A., & D'Andrea, M.J. (1998). *Community counseling: Empowerment strategies for a diverse society.* Pacific Grove, CA: Brooks/Cole Publishing Company.

Sodowsky, G.R., Kuo-Jackson, P.Y., & Loya, G.J. (1996). Outcome of training in the philosophy of assessment. In D.B. Pope-Davis & H.L.K. Coleman (Eds), *Multicultural counseling competencies: Assessment, education and training, and supervision,* (pp. 3-42). Thousand Oaks, CA: Sage Publications, Inc.

Sue, D.W., Arredondo, P., & McDavis, R.J. (1992). Multicultural counseling competencies and standards: A call to the profession. *Journal of Counseling and Development, 70,* 477-486.

Tomes, H. (1997, April). PI Directorate is home to controversy. *American Psychological Association Monitor, 28*(4), p. 4.

Toporek, R. L. & Liu, W. M. (in press). Advocacy in counseling psychology: Critical issues of race, class and gender. In Don B. Pope-Davis and Hardin L.K. Coleman (Eds.) *The Intersection of Race, Class and Gender in Counseling Psychology,* Thousand Oaks, CA: Sage.

Rebecca L. Toporek is a graduate student at the University of Maryland, College Park.

Chapter Two

Advocacy on behalf of African-American clients

By Jo-Ann Lipford Sanders

"...though it is sometimes very difficult to imagine our nation totally free of racism and sexism, my intellect, my heart and my experience tell me that it is actually possible. For that day when neither exists we must all struggle..."
— James Baldwin, African-American writer

The collective struggle suggested by James Baldwin is a compelling call for advocacy against racial and sexual oppression. As we think about African-American people, aspects of oppression are expanded to include racism, sexism, and classism. Tripartite oppression has impacted phases of life for African-Americans in the United States differently. However, "because of the pervasive institutional nature of racism in this country, no person of African descent has been able to fully escape the ravages of its grip" (Sanders, 1995). Racism, in all its aberrant and complex forms, includes more than skin color. Looking at the comprehensive nature of racism, one notices the intercorrelation between sexism, classism, and other intangible constructs. Skin color oppression (racism), most often used in oppressive actions against Americans with African ancestry, becomes the focus of this discourse.

Oppression is understood as a process which infuses prejudice with power. This power is then used to limit or hinder access to societal rights from those identified as lacking power. Advocacy is a process which defuses prejudice and attempts to redefine power by redistribution thus allowing for greater access for all. The goals are the betterment of the whole. The African proverb proclaiming "I Am Because We Are" could be a mantra for African-American advocacy.

Slavery in the United States

African-Americans are the largest group of "forced residents" to the United States in recorded history. A recent PBS documentary, *Africans in America: America's Journey Through Slavery,* chronicled African's subjugation to a myriad of cruelties associated with their transcontinental kidnapping and subsequent enslavement. Under slavery various African tribes were methodically stripped of family, language, music, religion, dietary, and grooming comforts. The brutality of the kidnapping, transport, and dehumanization of Africans in America worsened as skin color and physiognomy became the gauge for inhumane treatment. Inhumane treatment practices then became ingrained in a philosophy of "Black Inferiority," prevailing to date.

In 1903, W. E. B. DuBois, an African-American scholar prophesied "the problem of the twentieth century is the problem of the Color Line" (cited in Paschal & Bontemps, 1993, p. 263). Unfortunately, as we peer into the windows of the twenty-first century, African-Americans still struggle against the effects of "the color line." Note for example the recent findings of President Bill Clinton's Commission on Race, "It is, we believe, essential to recall the facts of racial domination... We as a nation need to understand that whites tend to benefit, either unknowingly or consciously from this country's history of white privilege" (*White Privilege*, 1998). This multiracial and multiethnic Commission reported, in 1998, that some Americans have easier access to societal resources, based on the color of their skin or racial identification, than others and that social disparities around race are profound enough to provide a focal point of their report.

History of Race Oppression for African-Americans

A comprehensive historical discussion of racial oppression is a significant discussion. The seeds of racial oppression grew from the Anglo Saxon myth of race superiority. The rationalization of the African slave system was enhanced by a Puritan view identifying civilized people as Christian and White. Slavery was really a societal dichotomy when considered against the backdrop of Puritan beliefs. To justify and resolute slavery, Africans had to be dehumanized to chattel. So the natural, logical, and moral objections to slavery were overcome because these chattel were needed for the economic advantages that the institution offered. The system dictated the need! Tripartite oppression thus became deeply rooted as systemic institutional racism, discrimination, psychological and educational racism, and is maintained by stereotyping, labeling, misinformation, racial scapegoating, and fear.

African-Americans are still faced with institutional structures that are willing to abate morals and values in deference to economic advantages for some. Institutions continue to pursue the economic objectives of slavery over the logical and moral issues associated with subjugation. Moral issues against discrimination and bigotry are clear but have been made subject to economic issues and the chattel concept. As long as institutions continue to serve economic interests of individuals in power, and can justify these interests from a "Black Inferiority" ideology, there will be a need for advocacy.

Advocacy is needed to overcome institutions that are willing to compromise morals and values for the powerful thereby dictating norms for the society at large.

Advocacy for African-American people must begin with an understanding and appreciation of the savagery of slavery and its continued residual effects.

Residual Effects of Race Oppression

Although the roots of race oppression have been covered by such categorical definitions as political correctness, time, institutionalization, and legislation, "The Doctrine of Black Inferiority" is as much an aspect of American culture today as is apple pie and baseball. Historical marginalization, systemic racism, and discriminatory practices against African-Americans are ingrained in the foundations of Western culture. Over the last several years African-Americans have litigated discriminatory practices against Texaco, Denny's restaurants, and Eddie Bauer clothiers. African-Americans still experience difficulty securing a taxi in such cosmopolitan cities as New York. Even winning the coveted green jacket of the Master's golf classic was not enough to quench the stench of "Black Inferiority." Who would have imagined that the seemingly kind gesture of a late-night ride home in small southern town would become a death ride for an unassuming, single Black father solely because of the color of his skin. Hate crimes against African-Americans, often attributable to youth, are rising! Could this suggest intergenerational transmission of "Black Inferiority" doctrine?

The residual effects of racism are displayed in more than

hate crimes. Because racism is endemic, it has become almost a cliché to blame a Black man for any number of crimes (Daniels, 1995). Take for example the young mother, Susan Smith, who reported that her children were abducted by a Black man; or the White Boston businessman named Charles Stuart who upon murdering his wife, reported a Black man did it, or even the inmate killed alongside Jeffrey Dahmer (who himself was convicted of killing and eating people of color), had accused a Black man of killing his wife. Most recently a priest stabbed himself in excess of 20 times only to accuse a Black man. Had not police investigators been committed to advocacy and fair play, Black men and indeed African-American communities would have been under a "state of siege."

Societal responses to diversity have been inappropriate. Institutional structures have a programmed response to diversity which is to devalue that which is different. This devaluing is built into such practices as "last hired, first fired," "most qualified," "scientific studies showing genetic deficiencies," "redlining" and "educational intelligence tests" all proving that African-Americans are both different and deficient.

Additionally, many African-Americans have also internalized the "Black Inferiority" into a personal self that is different and deficient. Internalized oppression is being manifested in self deprecating behaviors such as illegal drug use, soaring high school dropout rates, teenage pregnancies, and the color complex, to name a few.

Consequently, it is not enough to simply advocate for changes in direct service. Service providers, educators, mental health professionals, and the public at large must join, consciously acknowledge and tear down the "Great Hegemonic Wall of Race Superiority."

Advocacy Strategies to Assist African-Americans

Advocates for African-American people will be well served by understanding the atrocities of slavery and its prevailing ideology; but that is only half of the story! The strengths used by African- Americans to survive provide the nexus to advocacy.

Following are suggestions for ways in which teachers/ educators/counselors/ politicians and others might make systems work more effectively for African-American people infusing their strengths, customs, and culture:

1. Cultural Awareness is the first step. Advocates must know

themselves. To advocate against endemic constructs, one must have a personal conviction grounded from self analysis. Notice instances when you collude with tripartite oppression. Make opportunities for your views to be challenged and expanded. Unlearning oppression may initially be frightening, but it is liberating as you challenge the essence of who you are. To learn about African-Americans, why not familiarize yourself with African-American scholars. So much that has been known about African-American culture has been offered from someone "looking over into someone else's fence." Interrupt the "Doctrine of Inferiority" by noticing when you cannot accept the scholarship of African-Americans.

2. Encourage Self Advocacy. The mutual help or community of helpers concept is a familiar approach within African-American communities. This is an effort to empower African-Americans to serve as expert helpers while also seeing other African-Americans as competent and caring. It disputes internalized oppression and stereotyping regarding the ableness of African-Americans. Examples of self help groups currently operating within African-American communities are Rites of Passage programs, sickle cell disease mutual-help groups, The National Black Women's Health Project founded by Byllye Y. Avery that has established 50 self help groups in over 41 states, Mothers Against Gangs, Unwed Mothers United, NAACP, and the various tenant self-management organizations in public housing projects. Become aware of other self help groups within African-American communities and do not feel intimated to refer.

3. Accountable Training of Professionals. In a recent study (C. Bradley, personal communication, 1998) of 100 CACREP approved counseling programs only 33% required a multicultural training course prior to practicum. Practicums and internships for education and counseling need to provide incentives for working with African-American clients AND display at least beginning level cultural competence. This means practicum and internship students need to have mandatory requirements to work with African-American and other people of color built into the practicum and internship curriculum. Anyone providing services without knowledge and understanding of the counseling issues would be considered providing unethical care. Why

aren't those who attempt to work with ethnic groups for which they have limited or no knowledge and understanding not held to those same ethical standards?

4. Use resources within communities such as churches and civic leaders to help spread the message. For example, establish Peer Advocates. Befriend a group of African-American clergy. Clergy know their communities and are well respected as leaders within African-American communities. Consider including clergy or a clergy designee as a part of your counseling team.

5. Develop materials about mental health that are culturally appropriate and aggressively disseminate. Raise awareness via infusion in curriculums in schools, colleges, and universities. Raise awareness from a whisper to a full bravado. Make your classrooms, offices, and places of business compelling with pictures, magazines, and posters with African-American faces. Include images of more than sports heroes. Also include African-American scientists, inventors, teachers, poets, etc. Develop video resources with African-Americans for use in community outreach.

6. Come out of your offices (which often represent institutions of oppression) and into African-American communities. Become familiar and trusted. Attend community functions. Establish multiracial teams to be guest presenters. Don't always lecture but try experiential and team building activities to hear the concerns of the communities. Helping professionals and individuals with particular expertise may offer expertise within Black communities. Humphreys and Hamilton (1995) offer a caution about this training presentation, "when outside experts administer social services to communities, they often deprive them of control and produce apathy and alienation. Thus, even when a service is administered effectively by external agents, the meta-message remains, 'You have problems, the rest of us have the solutions.' This can lead service recipients to feel dependent and incompetent (p. 1)."

7. Challenge research and writings, teaching the universal normalcy of individualistic approaches to counseling. Challenge and push the definition of ethical practices which suggest that non-eurocentric mores are inappropriate, i.e., celebrate ethnic holidays at centers to familiarize community with agency; the healing effects of food for many cultures; or the relevance of indigenous supports. Include

emic perspectives of mental health.

8. Raise awareness as you sit in on group and individual supervisions in your private and public practices. Speak up when a colleague has not considered the cultural aspects of cases involving African-Americans. Challenge questionable diagnosis and treatment practices. In mental health settings, African-Americans are more often underserved and misdiagnosed than other clients.

9. Encourage educational professionals to provide accurate and inclusive instruction of American history to include the tremendous efforts of non-Whites and women. Invite African-Americans into classrooms/boardrooms/etc. other than during Black History month.

10. Demystify the stigma associated with race talks by encouraging debate and dialogue among school children, colleagues, family, and others. Become obnoxious and intolerant of the presence of tripartite oppression.

11. Befriend African-American women's groups, sororities, and social clubs. African-American women are the "pulse" of most African-American communities. No one has experienced the struggles over time quite like African-American women. Their unwavering persistence provides the greatest example of advocacy in history. Their sister-friend networks often are precursors to prepastoral counseling. African-American women have provided a roadmap for "doin' what ya' gotta do" to survive.

12. Support Affirmative Action and other anti-discrimination legislation. Lobby and provide information throughout your communities about affirmative action. Benefactors of this legislation must speak out when the laws are challenged. This is an example of hitting "The Wall". Phone or fax your senators' and your representative's offices. Call the US Capitol switchboard (202) 224-3121.

13. Seek more funds to do empirical research of all socioeconomic levels within the African-American community to provide a more adequate picture of the heterogeneity. Understand that there is no such thing as "the African-American community" but in fact African-American communities. African-American people are as diverse as were the kidnapped Africans from various tribes. Although joined by ancestry in Africa and the continual battle against tripartite oppression, their experiences are individual and unique. One-dimensional views of "all"

African-Americans are detrimental to appropriate care.
14. Become an active participant in the numerous "watch-dog" websites fighting for justice. When they notify you of impending legislation, respond. I have listed a few for your consideration. Visit the websites and become aware of the laws.
15. Encourage and advocate for the hiring and promotion of African-American educators, support staff, and admittance of African-Americans into master's and doctoral level programs. Doesn't it concern you when you look around a multicultural world and your clientele or classroom do not reflect this diversity? Inquire as to rationale.
16. Challenge educational curriculum, training of teachers, and testing efforts to reflect culturally reflective learning styles. Courtland Lee (1996) recounts the story of the birds sitting on a fence. The teacher asked the children, if three birds are sitting on a fence and one bird is shot off how many birds would be left? The American child answered "two" (convergent answer). The African child answered, "Not so. There would be none for if one bird is shot the others will fly away (divergent answer). Which answer is correct. The current way our educational system tests, ethnic groups which are structured around more convergent thinking often receive less encouragement.
17. Challenge standards which continue to perpetuate ethnocentrism. Don't be silent. Look for RIM's (racism interruption moments). Don't tolerate racial jokes, slurs, or the propagation of untruths or generalizations about "all Black people." Challenge the irrational. Write to your newspaper when you notice ethnocentrism in writing or reporting.
18. Fight institutions which discriminate against African-Americans. Don't patronize establishments that are unfair to Black people, and let the establishments know your thoughts.

History has shown that advocacy efforts are effective. African-Americans have shown that advocacy efforts are effective. The desegregation of public schools, integration in public places, seating on public transportation, finding adequate lodging, and securing entrance to college were all changed because of advocacy efforts. Political advocacy has a proven history of success in fighting for civil liberties, lobbying for entitlements for the disenfranchised, demanding access to public facilities, or litigating against discrimination practices for African-Americans. Don't become confused and mistaken about the mission of advocacy. African-American people are strong! African-American people are survivors! Advocates for African-American people seek to assist and assure equal footing for fair competition.

Become a pebble in oppression's shoe, irritate it until it stops to look and then Open up, Speak out, Take a risk, Refuse to accept privileges associated with oppression, and Challenge America to fully represent the "land of the free and the home of the brave." I recently heard a saying that struck my heart, "the smallest flea when strategically placed can bring down the largest dog" (Author Unknown). Strategically place yourself to bring down the walls of oppression affecting the lives of African-American people by advocating against tripartite oppression.

References

Daniels, L. A. (1995, February). The American way: Blame a Black man. *Emerge*, 60-67.

Humphreys, K. & Hamilton, E. G. (Winter, 1995). *Alternating themes: Advocacy and self reliance*. Social Policy

Lee, C. (1996). *Multicultural counseling: Moving from theory to practice*. Speech given at conference at Ohio University, Athens, Ohio.

Paschal, A. G. & Bontemps, A. (Eds.). (1993). *W.E. B. DuBois: A reader*. New York: Macmillan.

Sanders, R. G. W. (1995, October 3). Fuhrman was tip of iceberg. *Sandusky Register*, p. A-4.

"White privilege" cited as key to racial discord. (1998, September 18). *Sandusky Register*, p. A-3.

Recommended Readings

Billingsley, A. (1968). *Black families in White America*. Englewood Cliffs, NY: Prentice Hall.

Boyd-Franklin, N. (1989). *Black families in therapy: A multisystems approach*. New York: Guilford Press.

Franklin, J. H. (1974). *From slavery to freedom* (4th ed). New York: Alfred A. Knopf.

Hill, R. B. (1971). *The strengths of Black families*. New York: Emerson Hall.

Recommended Resources

- www.bazelon.org/bazelon/ mltog.html (Bazelon Center for Mental Health Law)

- www.shakey.net/advoc.html (Advocacy Watch-dog Group)

- www.imhl.com/advocacyproject.html (Advocacy Watch-dog Group)

- www.nagnotts.demon.co.uk/ advocate.htm

- Foundation of Advocacy for Mental Health, Inc. (518) 434-0439 ext. 22

- African-American Community Health Advisory Committee (415) 696-4678

- www.mhasp.org/policy/advalt.html (Public Policy Information and Advocacy Alerts) Mental health Assoc. of Southeastern PA

- The Advocacy Project, Granby Community Mental health Group, Liverpool England. Tel 0151-709-9442; Fax: 0151-709-0004

Jo-Ann Lipford Sanders is an assistant professor in the counseling department at Heidelberg College and a licensed professional counselor in private practice in Tiffin, Ohio.

Chapter Three

Challenging Linguicism: Action Strategies for Counselors and Client-Colleagues

By Stuart F. Chen-Hayes, Mei-whei Chen, and Naveeda Athar

"The Chicano, New Mexican, and Mexican history — the silenced American history that I finally did learn and the Spanish language that I now covet — was almost lost to the American dream of white supremacy. My language and cultural education have not been because of my schooling but in spite of it" (Chavez Chavez, 1997, p. 7).

"This is the oppressor's languages (sic) yet I need it to talk to you'...Adrienne Rich's words. Then, when I first read these words, and now, they make me think of standard English, of learning to speak against black vernacular, against the ruptured and broken speech of a dispossessed and displaced people. Standard English is not the speech of exile. It is the language of conquest and domination; in the United States, it is the mask which hides the loss of so many tongues, all those sounds of diverse, native communities we will never hear, the speech of the Gullah, Yiddish, and so many other unremembered tongues. Reflecting on Adrienne Rich's words, I know that it is not the English language that hurts me, but what the oppressors do with it, how they shape it to become a territory that limits and defines, how they make it a weapon that can shame, humiliate, colonize" (bell hooks, 1994, pp. 167-168).

Linguicism was first defined as "linguistically related racism" in the early 1990s by Danish linguist, Dr. Robert Phillipson (1992). Dr. Phillipson and his colleague, Dr. Tove Skutnabb-Kangas, have spent their careers advocating for linguistic human rights. Although having existed for a long time, linguicism was not recognized as a form of discrimination until recently. As Sethi (1998) states:

> "It is only since 1992 that the Courts have begun to realize the legitimacy of discrimination based upon accent. Immigrants...suffer heightened racism because of their accents, including job discrimination and perpetual taunting and caricaturization. This is a severe and pervasive form of racism that is often not acknowledged as racist, or even offensive" (p. 156).

As professional counselors, counselor educators, and client-colleagues (Ivey, 1995), we have experienced the pain and oppression of linguicism in our own lives and in the lives of our family members, students, colleagues, and clients. In this paper, we present ideas, guidelines, and resources for advocating against linguicism. In terms of advocacy, we use a more specific definition of linguicism. We define linguicism as prejudice multiplied by power used by members of dominant language groups against members of non-dominant language groups (Chen-Hayes, 1998).

Although found worldwide, linguicism in the United States will be the focus of this paper. Historically, evidence of linguicism has been found since the beginning of the country. The United States has had implicit and explicit policies elevating English and devaluing other languages. The policies were evidenced by the scholarship of James Crawford, who has written numerous books on how English has been used to attack poor and working class persons and peoples of color in the United States over the decades.

Several recent examples of linguicism in counseling help to bring this home. When one of the authors, who is White, and his partner, who is Chinese, waited in line for registration at the 1998 ACA World Conference in Indianapolis, the author didn't expect anything unusual. The woman asked for his name, and he said, "Chen-Hayes." She came back saying she couldn't find it. He explained that, due to a recent name change, it might still be under "Hayes." She came back with the registration in hand, and ignoring his partner, said only to him, "Why would anyone want to change their name to a CHINESE name?" Shocked, he replied, "Because it's the right thing to do. It's a way of honoring both of us and our families as one." As painful as this incident of linguicism was, it is a common occurrence throughout the U.S. and elsewhere when members of a dominant language group use their power and resources to restrict access to resources by persons who speak a non-dominant language or speak a dominant language with an accent, or in this case, for persons who have a surname reflecting a non-dominant language or culture.

One of the authors had a male friend who was interviewed by phone for a job in a counselor education program. An interviewer asked if he had adequate English skills to be understood. The candidate, a person of Southeast Asian ethnicity who had graduated from a counselor education program and was currently employed full-time as a counselor educator at another institution, felt humiliated to be asked this question by a faculty member who apparently was unaware of her own linguicism. Hurt by the linguicism, the candidate subsequently withdrew from the search due to such demeaning treatment. Another colleague at a different institution, a multilingual woman of color, has had consistently excellent teaching and peer evaluations. Her department chair, however, criticized her English skills, when according to the experiences and evaluations of colleagues and students, her English skills are exemplary.

If these three examples demonstrate how counselor educators are treated in our profession, what's happening to our students, client-colleagues, and our families and communities? What is happening is common: Speaking a language other than English or speaking English with an accent or dialect is often dismissed as improper, unintelligent, or even illegal.

Following are more examples of linguicism in counseling and counselor education:

- Most counseling programs, materials, presentations, evaluation criteria, teaching, professional association materials, etc. are expected to be done in standard English with little or no accommodation or recognition of other language backgrounds.
- Little or no opportunity for professional counselors in training or beyond to pursue training in a second or third language; credentialing standards don't address language.
- Multicultural counseling has focused primarily on ethnicity and race, with little attention to how language is a critical cultural variable for dominant and non-dominant language speakers in the counseling process.
- Counselors have similar biases to non-counselors in

that most counselors perceive English to be the best or only "proper" language for counseling.

- Counseling students and/or faculty may perceive nonnative English speakers as lacking in skills, intelligence, or ability when the bias reflects the attitude of the English speaker, rather than the deficiency of the nonnative person.
- Non-dominant language speaking client-colleagues are less likely to seek services for fear that they will be misunderstood or discounted.
- Little or no training in how to work ethically with translators when language difference is significant. Do the translators understand confidentiality? Can it be enforced?
- Counselors may not be prepared to understand the subtle biases of linguicism that occur in daily living situations...phone conversations, interactions in shopping or on campus where nonnative speakers or persons who speak English with a dialect are often perceived as immature, ignorant, or less worthy than standard English speakers.
- Counselor trainees may be less likely to be selected for sites where their language background may be perceived as negative.
- Some counselors romanticize the idea that speaking with an accent can indeed gain an easier time with counseling because of the accent.
- Potential hiring of faculty and admission of students may be biased against non-dominant speakers of English; few bilingual or multilingual faculty exist in Counselor Education programs.
- ESL programs often are biased toward losing or discounting one's language/culture of origin and favor assimilating the nonnative speaker into the dominant culture/language.
- Lack of support for the variations in English dialects. Lack of awareness of how dialects may interfere with a non-dominant speaker's understanding of the language, and therefore, lessen the effectiveness of counseling/teaching interactions. Examples include: Black English, southern drawls, and the rapid speaking rate found in parts of the Northeastern United States.

- Use of pace and rate that overwhelm a non-dominant speaker.
- Unwillingness on the part of dominant English speakers to recognize their own bias toward "blaming the victim" — when non-dominant speakers are targeted for mistreatment because of the dominant speaker's insensitivity, bias, or ignorance.
- Misunderstandings of class assignments, where the instructor or supervisor makes assumptions that the message sent was clearly understood or received, and only later does the instructor or supervisor realize that she or he has erred and that a person of non-dominant language background has misunderstood the directions for the assignment or counseling practice.

Deconstructing Unearned Privilege Through Advocacy

To operationalize multicultural competencies for counselors, as Arrendondo et al. (1996) point out, we need to affirm languages and bilingualism, to question and challenge dominant culture/ language, and to consider how these variables may affect nondominant-language client-colleagues. In challenging linguicism in culturally competent ways, we have developed a working list of Standard English Privilege for persons who speak fluent English without accents or dialects. Standard English Privilege are unearned privileges that are conferred on members of the dominant language culture. Although often conferred without dominant language speakers' knowledge or consent, these are unearned privileges similar to the concept of White privilege (McIntosh, 1998). The section that follows depicts a partial list of Standard English Privilege:
- Standard English speakers usually can be assured that they will be surrounded by other English speakers at home, at work, and at play.
- Standard English speakers usually can be assured that the major media—newspapers, magazines, books, TV, e-mail, and computers and will all be in English.
- When standard English speakers travel, they usually can be assured that signage, brochures, and information stations will all carry English language materials.
- Standard English speakers usually, for educational purposes, can be assured that standard English will

be the modality of giving instructions, in creating and dissemination educational projects, and in assessing one's educational knowledge (testing).

- In the assessment of mental and physical health, standard English speakers usually can find providers who speak English and who will assess their needs and concerns using tests and diagnostic tools based in English and develop appropriate treatment plans and referrals based on English language concepts.

The list could continue. However, in making this list, we are not blaming standard English speakers for their privilege. Instead, we call upon standard English speakers to be advocates against linguicism and use their privilege to challenge other standard English speakers by interrupting linguicism in the following ways:

- Become fluent in a language other than English and encourage your friends and coworkers to do the same.
- Encourage children and youth to be bilingual/multilingual.
- Ensure that school programs have instruction in multiple languages throughout the curriculum.
- Encourage mental health and other public agencies, as well as grade school and higher educational teaching and counseling programs, to offer services and coursework in languages in addition to English. This is to (1) promote the well-being of current and future students, educators, families, and communities; (2) to honor the linguistic diversity that has been and continues to be in the United States (and globally); and (3) to increase the employability of graduates of our educational institutions.
- Ensure that practicum and internship classes provide opportunities for students and educators to practice various affirming linguistic techniques/traditions with their students and client-colleagues.
- Develop world wide web pages in multiple languages; work to have journals and other forms of media (newspapers, magazines, radio, and television) translated into languages in addition to English.
- Signage at community conferences, workshops, keynotes, and regular addresses should include live translation as part of the offering in multiple languages.
- Assist organizations/agencies/schools in developing a

resource base of all members/students/families/groups who have fluency/language proficiency for translation purposes and to make these services accessible to community members.

- Assist organizations/agencies/schools to create language-sensitive materials and organize publicity efforts that promote multilingual awareness and challenge linguicism by affirming the strengths of multiple language learning.
- Assume that in good communication a message needs to be sent in multiple ways; just because it is sent in one dominant language doesn't mean that it is effective. Ask questions to clarify and encourage persons to respond.
- Listen to the needs and desires of nondominant English speakers and English speakers who use a dialect or accent. These collaborative efforts work toward community empowerment and solutions, which allows self-determination amongst nondominant speakers.
- If annoyed with a nondominant English speaker's language, accent, or communication style, work not to blame the victim. Instead, challenge yourself about the work you can do to develop empathy and appreciation for cultural variations and linguistic differences.

One of the counseling interventions we propose when working with a client-colleague who is not a native speaker of English is to ask her/him to talk at times in the native language — so we can see and hear the nonverbals, the gestures, the tone, the rate, the pacing — and then ask them to explain how the feelings occur in the native language versus the dominant language. This small exercise deeply honors the client-colleague in multiple ways:

- It affirms the culture of origin and issues of acculturation.
- It affirms that English only conveys part of a client-colleague's issues.
- It affirms bilingualism and biculturalism for counselor and client-colleague.
- It equalizes the power balance by allowing the client-colleague to demonstrate cultural pride and expertise.
- It ensures fewer mistakes on the part of the counselor who misattributes or misinterprets from their own linguistic/cultural/world view framework

At times of greatest stress or other concerns, speaking in one's native language can be a relief and a stress-reducing factor if both parties are open to translation assistance afterward.

Systemic Challenges to Linguicism

It's time to address linguicism on multiple fronts. There are many ways to be systemic advocates against linguicism. We, especially those of us who have Standard English Privileges based on speaking English without an accent or dialect, can be allies to persons oppressed by linguicism. We can all push for the following concepts to curtail linguicism:

- Support bilingual education and challenge the movements to end it, such as California's Proposition 227. There is no credible evidence that bilingual education harms anyone or reduces the likelihood of dominant language acquisition.
- Share information about the benefits of bilingual and multilingual persons in terms of cultural competencies and cognitive complexity.
- Interrupt acts of linguicism and give accurate information about persons who speak nondominant languages or speak English with an accent or dialect.
- Develop second or third language skills to increase your language and cultural competencies.
- Challenge educational institutions and programs (including counselor education) to emphasize the importance of hiring faculty, support staff, and in admitting students with fluency in two or more languages and various English dialects (Ponterotto et al., 1995).
- Ask that educational and mental health agency information — written and spoken — be available in languages in addition to English, especially Spanish, Chinese, Polish, and other languages where large numbers of immigrants who attend are most comfortable in their mother tongue.
- Use the test of reasonable opposites. For example, when a dominant language speaker makes fun of a nondominant speaker's accent ask, "So how many fluent sentences of my language can you speak?" "So why is it that some persons who speak only one language feel superior to those who speak two or more languages?"
- Work with client-colleagues to challenge linguicistic legislation at the state level, for example propositions that restrict or eliminatebilingual education or that insist on

"English" only, and what has been discussed for Puerto Rico by the U.S. House members if it were to become the 51st state.

- Advocate for the including language as a category needing protection due to hate crimes, bias, or both.
- Advocate for keeping records on incidents of hate crimes or job discrimination toward persons who don't speak English or do so with an accent.
- Push educators to teach that the United States has always been a multilingual country and to teach the history of our multilingual origin (what language were we three votes away from speaking in the 1700s? German!)
- Encourage all children and adults and counselors in training to be bilingual. Encourage schools to adopt second and third language requirements early on in elementary school to improve brain power and to appreciate diverse cultures through learning different languages.

Counseling professionals have believed in empowering people subjugated by various forms of oppression. Yet, the existence of linguicism within our field reflects a discrepancy between the belief and the action as Arredondo et al. (1996) state.

A person speaking English with an accent might be assumed to be less intelligent, more difficult to deal with, or viewed in other negative ways. Oftentimes, immigrant adults experience the impatience and even the ridicule of monolingual English speakers when they seek services at a human service agency (p. 48).

Facing this discrepancy, we are honored to begin the dialogue about linguicism with professional counselors, client-colleagues, counselor educators, and members of the public. We hope the ideas in this paper will prompt more discussion and advocate effort against linguicism. We look forward to extending this discussion on multiple fronts, including forthcoming Spanish, Chinese, and Urdu translations of this text.

References

Arredondo, P., Toporek, R., Brown, S. P., Jones, J., Locke, D. C., Sanchez, J., & Stadler, H. (1996). Operationalization of the multicultural counseling competencies. *Journal of Multicultural Counseling and Development, 24,* 42-78.

Chavez, R. (1997). A curriculum discourse for achieving equity: Implications for teachers when engaged with Latina and Latino students. Washington, D.C.: Hispanic Dropout Project.

Chen-Hayes, S. F. (1998). Class handout on definitions of multiple oppressions.

Hooks, b. (1994). *Teaching to transgress: Education as the practice of freedom.* New York, NY: Routledge.

Ivey, A. E. (1995). Psychotherapy as liberation: Toward specific skills and strategies in multicultural counseling and therapy. In Ponterotto, J. G., et al, *Handbook of multicultural counseling* (pp. 53-72). Thousand Oaks, CA: Sage.

McIntosh, P. (1998). White Privilege: Unpacking the invisible knapsack. In Rothenberg, P. S., *Race, class, and gender in the United States: An integrated study.* New York, NY: St. Martin's Press.

Phillipson, R. (1992). *Linguistic imperialism.* Oxford University Press.

Ponterotto, J. G., Alexander, C. M., & Grieger, I. (1995). A multicultural competency checklist for counseling training programs. *Journal of Multicultural Counseling and Development, 23,* 11-20.

Sethi, R. C. (1998). Smells like racism. In Rothenberg, P. S., *Race, class, and gender in the United States: An integrated study* (pp. 154-164). New York, NY: St. Martin's Press.

Zinn, H. (1995). *A people's history of the United States: 1492-present,* (Rev. ed.). New York: HarperCollins.

Stuart Chen-Hayes is an assistant professor at Lehman College of the City University of New York. Mei-whei Chen is an assistant professor at Northeastern Illinois University in Chicago. Naveeda Athar is a graduate student at National-Louis University in Wheaton, Ill.

Recommended Reading

Andrzejeski, J. (Ed.). *Oppression and social justice: Critical frameworks*, (Fifth ed.). Needham Heights, MA: Simon & Schuster.

Lorde, A. (1984). *Sister outsider.* Freedom, CA: The Crossing Press.

McWhirter, E. H. (1994). *Counseling for empowerment.* Alexandria, VA: American Counseling Association.

Recommended Websites

* Linguistic human rights; Challenging linguicism and linguistic imperialism

Dr. Tove Skutnabb-Kangas &/or Dr. Robert Phillipson
Dept. of Language and Culture, Roskilde University, Denmark

Dr. Phillipson's website is: http://babel.ruc.dk/~robert/

Dr. Skutnabb-Kangas' website may be accessed at a link on Dr. Phillipson's website (or vice versa; they are linguistic experts and colleagues). Their scholarship is ground-breaking; they coined the terms linguicism and linguistic imperialism and are perhaps the world's leading advocates for linguistic human rights.

*History and challenging dominant language policy in the United States:

James Crawford, a writer, editor and language policy activist
Website: "Language policy website and emporium"
http://ourworld.compuserve.com/homepages/JWCRAWFORD/home.htm

Crawford has written numerous books and articles that are available at this site. His writing and activism evidence an excellent history of linguicism and language policy as it has been used in the United States to benefit English speakers and persons of dominant racial and social class identities at the expense of persons of color and poor and working class persons.

Chapter Four

Advocacy for Native American Indian and Alaska Native Clients and Counselees

By Roger Herring

Helping professionals need to be more informed and more active advocates for proactive counseling strategies with Native American Indian and Alaska Native peoples. This paper will address the major advocacy needs of these populations. The terms "Native" and "Natives" are used when referring to both groups.

The negative impact of historical and contemporary discriminatory policies and practices on Native peoples has devastated their standard of living and created major cultural conflicts. As Herring (in press) has summarized, the current plight of Native peoples is tremendous: (a) death from alcoholism is six times greater and terminal liver cirrhosis is 14 times greater than the general population; (b) suicide rates are twice that of the national average; (c) average income is 75 percent less than European Americans; (d) unemployment is 10 times the national average; (e) dropout rates are higher and educational attainment is the lowest of any ethnic group; (f) infant mortality after the first three months of life is three times the national average; and (g) delinquency and mental illness far surpass most other ethnic groups.

These influences have combined with substandard housing, malnutrition, inadequate health care, shortened life expectancy, and high suicide rates to limit opportunities for educational attainment (LaFromboise & Graff Low, 1998) by a population classified as the "poorest of the poor" in this nation. To further complicate matters, many Native individuals believe that they have no choice or control in their lives. However, these problems are not insurmountable nor are Native individuals only victims and incapable of improving their lives. In reality, thousands of Native people have overcome their personal plights. The increase in the number and strength of advocacy efforts is having an effect.

Advocacy strategies to assist Native American Indians and Alaska Natives

The hope is that the delivery of mental health services to Native peoples will be improved during the next decade. To reinforce that hope, four areas of advocacy must be addressed: (a) the political agendas of Native peoples must be expanded, (b) the training of helping professionals must be improved, (c) the delivery of services or practice needs attention, and (d) research agendas need to be redirected.

Advocacy for Expanding the Political Agenda

The future prospects for Native populations, especially those on reservations, is hinged on the political agendas of the U.S. Congress which funds and administers the Bureau of Indian Affairs (BIA), the Indian Health Service (IHS), and the Office of Indian Education (OIE). More political efforts are needed to increase the awareness of congressional leaders regarding the realities of Native life.

The recurrent theme in the Native struggle for greater political recognition is education. Native voter education plus education of public officials equals greater Native political power. A major concern is the election and appointment of public officials who are sensitive to Native issues and concerns. Tribal governments must assume a more active advocacy in becoming actively involved in professional/ governmental organizations and in pressuring tribal elders to become involved in political/social organizations.

Professional Training Programs

Two basic issues are included in the training of mental health professionals:
  (a) the need for increased numbers of Native mental health practitioners, and
  (b) the increased efforts to ensure that non-Native practitioners are adequately trained to work with Native populations (Herring, in press).

Recruitment and Training of Native Students. Advocacy for the following points is required if the numbers of Native helping professionals are to be increased:

- Native students should be acquainted with the benefits of pursuing mental health careers; and recruitment of native students needs to be increased.
- Training programs need to revise their curricula to include the impact of culture on clients and counselees.
- Training programs need to revise their curricula to include the impact of history and environment on Native clients and counselees.
- Training programs need to revise their curricula to include the impact of the degree of acculturation present in Native clients and counselees.
- Training programs should include Native community-based practica and internships.
- Training programs should emphasize building on Native clients' and counselees' strengths while helping them maintain vital memberships in social networks.
- Training programs need to prepare additional personnel in culturally sensitive geriatric care for elderly and disabled Native individuals.

Training of Non-Native Practitioners. The burden of responsibility of providing ethnic appropriate training for pre-service helping professionals rests on the shoulders of those involved in such education. Training programs must make some attempt to educate their non-Native students about Native populations. They need to be aware of the stereotypes, historical genocide, within-group variances, levels of acculturation, value and belief systems, and other pertinent information regarding this population.

Advocacy for Implications for Practice

The need for trained professionals who understand Native views of mental health and who provide appropriate experiences remains paramount. Many programs and efforts have provided evidence of progress. However, a sense of urgency exists (e.g., lower achievers, STDs, teenage pregnancy, and learning problems) that immediate action is needed to improve Native youth's lives and futures.

Similar conditions affect Native adults and Native elderly. Their plight is also pervasive and must be addressed. Action taken now has the potential for success whereas failure to respond or a mediocre response will result in more Native peoples being at risk and those already at risk receiving little substantive help.

General Issues and Concerns. On the basis of a belief in the importance of acculturation, social and professional experiences with Native peoples, and the literature with regard to counseling Native peoples, helping professionals are encouraged to advocate for the following (Herring, in press):

- Some Native individuals may respond more appropriately to interventions if traditional healers are involved in the process.
- The use of the extended family offers tremendous potential.
- Consideration needs to be given to differences in communication styles, perceptions of trustworthiness, gender roles, and support networks.
- Extreme caution is needed in the use of standardized tests.

Native Women's Issues. In addition, advocacy for the issues and concerns of Native women in counseling is important, such as the following (Herring, in press):

- To appreciate the strengths (e.g., long-term coping mechanisms of victimized women) and adaptations of Native women;
- To emphasize the importance of tradition and ritual and the need for reexamination of the subtle dynamics of sex bias, gender role, and cultural stereotyping in therapy with Native women; and
- To increase the number of community caregivers (both Native and non-Native, on and off reservations).

The Older Native Individual with Disabilities. Nearly 8.5 percent of Native peoples were 60 years of age or older and about 20.5 percent are 45 years of age or older (U.S. Bureau of the Census, 1992). Quality of life is a tremendous concern for this population. Human service and health care professionals concerned in their practice with the issue of Native aging must advocate:

- to enhance the quality of life a Native elder experiences (e.g., improved housing, basic health care, greater economic security);
- to serve Native individuals at a younger age than non-Natives;
- to provide outreach services to the older Native population, rather than expect, or demand, that he or

she will come to the office;

- to use the informal networks of Native peoples (i.e., extended family);
- to provide transportation to services when necessary; and
- to assist with appropriate and necessary vocational services.

Implications for Research

Research involving Native subjects should be based on their value and belief systems. Researchers cannot assume they possess sensitivity just because they are Native, since the within-group variances of Native populations are too diverse. In addition, traditional Native peoples are frequently suspicious of scientific research and non-Native researchers due to negative past experiences (i.e., forced assimilation through boarding schools and land allotment. Research efforts involving Native populations imply the need for advocacy in these areas (Choney, Berryhill-Paapke, & Robbins, 1995; Herring, in press):

- to avoid placing all Native groups into a single group classification when concentrating on Native problems;
- to avoid research which is written from a male perspective that portrays Native women as "drudges" or "matriarchal matrons" or in the "princess/squaw" derogatory manner;
- to improve theoretical knowledge;
- to challenge research from non-Natives that purports many "truths" about Native peoples; and
- to respond to the urgent need for academic research created and conducted by Native researchers, rather than non-Native ethnic perspectives.

Research Relative to Acculturation Levels. The degree of acculturation will continue to be an inalienable variable in the helping process of Native youth and adults. To that end, the need to advocate for the following suggestions for research involving acculturation levels exists (Choney et al., 1995):

- to develop a means of measuring acculturation that accounts for the multifaceted nature of the process (i.e., across spiritual, cognitive, affective, and behavioral domains);
- to avoid making value judgments about the health status of the cultural response of any particular group;
- to develop group or individual "acculturation profiles;"

and
- to discard the myth that acculturation is a naturally occurring and unidirectional force.

Research Relative to Scientific Inquiry. In addition to the important variable of acculturation, the area of empirical data relative to Native populations needs to be addressed as well. Suggestions for specific advocacy in research with Native populations include efforts (Choney et al., 1995):
- to collaborate with Native community leaders in joint efforts;
- to assess the applicability of specific counseling techniques;
- to meet the potential of Native mental health research; and
- to stress the identification of variables cogent to adaptive functioning.

Research Relative to Gender Roles. In the area of gender roles and issues among Native populations, the following emphases for advocacy are offered (LaFromboise & Graff Low, 1998):
- to increase research on the link between mental health and role conflict related to the family and the community;
- to add research on anxiety disorders and posttraumatic stress disorder;
- to increase knowledge of the factors that contribute to depression; and
- to increase the relevance of diagnostic instruments with women.

Recommended Resources

Readers are cautioned to be alert to the authenticity of materials purporting to be written by Native authors or containing information about Native peoples. Current materials should reflect contemporary Native people lives, not as they existed 100 years ago (e.g., Hollywood movies historically have misportrayed Native peoples and lifestyles). More recent movies are empathic, use Native actors, and reveal the uniqueness of Native life (e.g., *Lakota Woman*, 1994; *Children of the Dust*, 1995). Ethnic appropriate films/videos may be purchased or rented from Insight Media, 2162 Broadway, New York, NY 10024; 800-233-9910. Tiller's (1996) *Guide to Indian country: Economic profiles of American Indian reservations* (Albuquerque, NM: Bow Arrow Publishing) provides information about every reservation, rancheria, and Alaska Native village in the United States.

For general knowledge, the following may be consulted:

Cahape, P., & Howley, C. B. (1992). *Indian nations at risk: Listening to the people*. Charleston, WV: Appalachia Educational Laboratory (ERIC Clearinghouse on Rural Education & Small Schools).

Callahan, C. M., & McIntire, J. A. (1994). *Identifying outstanding talent in American Indian and Alaska Native students*. Washington, DC: Office of Educational Research and Improvement.

Unlearning "Indian" Stereotypes, Stereotypes in U.S. History Books, CIBS Resource Center, 1841 Broadway, Room 300, New York, NY 10023.

In addition, many Native entities have their own websites.

References and resources

Choney, S. K., Berryhill-Paapke, E, & Robbins, R. R. (1995). The acculturation of American Indians: Developing frameworks for research and practice. In J.G. Ponterotto, J. M. Casas, L. A. Suzuki, & C. M. Alexander (Eds.), *Handbook of multicultural counseling* (pp. 73-92). Thousand Oaks, CA: Sage.

Herring, R. D. (in press). *Counseling Native American Indians and Alaska Natives: Synergetic Strategies for Helping Professionals*. Thousand Oaks, CA: Sage.

LaFromboise, T.D., & Graff Low, K. (1998). American Indian children and adolescents. In J.T. Gibbs, L.N. Huang and Associates, *Children of Color: Psychological interventions with culturally diverse youth* (pp. 112-142). San Francisco: Jossey-Bass.

U.S. Bureau of the Census. (1992). *Statistical abstract of the United States* (112th ed.). Washington, DC: U.S. Government Printing Office.

Roger Herring is a professor of educational leadership at the University of Arkansas-Little Rock.

Chapter Five

Empowerment Strategies from Latino/ Latina Perspectives

Patricia Arredondo and Luis Vázquez

"When I'm out with workers, they teach me every single day. It's an amazing thing. Obviously I don't know everything, I just know a little bit. But still the workers teach me every single day as I teach them. The second thing I know from experience is that whenever a critical situation hits us, the best source of power, the best source of hope is straight from the people." (1974, p. 521)

The words of Cesar Chavez are indicative of the humble and respectful attitude many Latinos are taught as children. Look to others, don't be arrogant, and value the relationship are admonitions communicated by parents and grandparents throughout one's youth and sometimes even as one is an adult. *Personalismo* is the concept and value that underlies interpersonal behavior. Though not easy to translate literally, it is about valuing and appreciating the person, an attitude that is taught and reinforced so that it becomes internalized over time.

There are two or three other terms we want to mention that are embedded in Latino culture. These are *orgullo*/pride, *respeto*, and *dignidad*, signifying the qualitative nature of interpersonal relationships. The prevailing worldview also reflects collectivism, interdependence, and high regard for authority and position. Thus, when it comes to empowerment strategies from Latino/Latina perspectives, counselors need to have an awareness and knowledge about cultural values that influence communication patterns, interpersonal relationships, and the individual's sense of self-determination. In addition, counselors must also be knowledgeable about how these values interact with different dimensions of identity including gender, class, sexual orientation, religious or spiritual beliefs, generational differences, and ethnic group differences (Arredondo, et al., 1996).

Latinos is a plural, encompassing gender-based term. In certain discussions, Latino/s may be used to refer only to men. Latinas is only used in reference to women. Hispanic is the term used by the United States government, though it is often rejected by Latinos/as.

Who are Latinos?

One answer is that we are the fastest growing cultural group in the United States with the youngest population of youth 18 years of age and under. We are a highly heterogeneous and very complex population. While we can be characterized collectively as originating from Spanish-speaking countries, predominantly of Mexican, Puerto Rican and Cuban heritage, there is an increasing presence of Latinos from Central and South America and the Caribbean Islands. Latinos prefer to self-identify by their ethnic membership, be it Colombian, Spanish, or Guatemalan.

In addition to the cultural and ethnic differences, Latinos' "racial" mixture may also have a major impact on life opportunities and stressors that they experience in the United States. We represent Caucasian, Mongoloid, Negroid, or a combination of these racial groupings (Casas & Vasquez, 1996). The inherent phenotypic characteristics of these various combinations can and often do have a great impact on the life opportunities of the Latino population (Vázquez, L.A., García-Vázquez. E., Bauman, S.A., & Sierra, A.S., 1997). Other factors to consider are socio-economic status, educational attainment, acculturation level, actual and perceived power, and self-entitlement . Chacón, Cohen, Camarena, Gonzalez, & Strover (1985) found that even though many of these differences exist between and within the Latino groups, there are also gender differences based on cultural socialization practices and religious beliefs. Latina women have a higher unemployment rate and lower educational level than their Latino men counterparts. For counselors, it is also important to understand the concepts of *machismo* and *marianismo* and how these cultural frameworks influence gender-based behavior.

Cultural competence means considering contextual and situational life stressors generally experienced by Latino populations. Counselors must be prepared to assess out-group status, social isolation, marginal social status, and status inconsistencies in the context of the presenting issues for counseling. The assessment of these areas for Latino clients sets the stage for appropriate process and desired goals for treatment.

Empowerment from Latino/a Perspectives

Broadly speaking, clinicians have varying perspectives on empowerment. McWhirter (1991, p.222) described it as a "conceptual framework that can be applied across a variety of counseling interventions." In a discussion about promoting the empowerment of women through counseling, the following description was offered:

Empowerment embodies knowledge, clarity and flexibility of thinking, self-confidence, and positive self-esteem in many forms and expressions. It is within the individual and generates a sense of personal power and self-authorization. Empowerment involves on-going learning processes that facilitate change, growth and functional relationships (Arredondo, 1991).

The concept of empowerment when applied to working with individual Latinos would of necessity have to be flexible. The myriad of variables and contextual factors discussed above describe the need for complexity of thinking and planning. However, there are cultural values that need to be referenced in relation to empowerment. They are respeto, personaliso, dignidad, and collectivism. To facilitate an individual's empowerment with cultural competency, these values must always be considered. Inherent in these values are counseling behaviors that demonstrate mutuality, collaboration, and interdependency.

When considering empowerment strategies, counselors can also use the Multicultural Counseling Competencies (Sue, Arredondo, and McDavis, 1992 and Arredondo, et al., 1996). They provide essential guidelines that will likely lead to more successful cross-cultural encounters. Consider the following examples and the possible approaches for empowering Latino/Latina clients.

Case Examples

Elena came to the United States mainland from Puerto Rico to study art. She earned a BA in the midst of her parent's divorce, and found a job immediately upon graduation. When Elena came to counseling, she expressed concerns about job satisfaction, a boyfriend who was more like a brother, and the well-being of her younger brothers in Puerto Rico. Despite her highly rational demeanor, she seemed overwhelmed and lonely at the same time.

She talked about feeling isolated and wanted medication to help her feel less anxious.

Edwin was referred for counseling by the Department of Rehabilitation because of indications of depression. A 35-year-old father of two, he became disabled through a work accident. He walked, seemingly with considerable pain, and had to sit upright in a straight-back chair. His wife of 10 years worked 60 hours a week at two jobs to ensure the basic family necessities. Edwin held on to the hope that he would someday be able to return to full-time employment. In the meantime, he experienced mixed feelings: self-loathing because he could not work, and resentment toward his wife who seemed to enjoy her second job working as a cleaning person at a television studio. Edwin demonstrated initiative and care for his children by connecting with a local Catholic priest and enrolling his children in the neighborhood school. Still, he lamented the limitations of his condition and what it meant for the future.

Francisca was a 50 year old immigrant woman from Guatemala employed by a major hospital in the food service department. Because she had healthcare insurance, she was referred to a Latina clinician in private practice. Her manager indicated that Francisca complained about leg pains and tiredness. A physical exam yielded nothing unusual about her health. She lived alone, sent most of her earnings home to a son who was in dentistry school, and socialized infrequently. At her first visit, Francisca wanted to engage in *plática* or small talk, inquiring about the therapist's ethnic background and parents.

Analysis and Discussion from Latino/a Perspectives

In the first example, there are several issues to consider before partnering with Elena to develop empowerment strategies. Elena left a cultural society in Puerto Rico where she was part of the majority population and entered a cultural society in mainland United States possibly identified with a minority status. As a Latina with a Bachelor's degree, it sets her apart from the majority of the Latina population in the United States. Her ability to live away from her parents to receive an education is an indication of her level of independence and a sign that the relationship with her parents is less traditional. For many Latinas in traditional households, the parents do not allow such distance from the nuclear and extended family. Elena was also able to be successful even though her parents were getting a divorce. This indicates stamina and self-sufficiency although, from a more culturally traditional perspective, moving home at this time might have been more appropriate. It is possible that her earning power on the mainland gave her an opportunity to contribute financially to her family's household depending on the circumstances of the divorce. However, her possible job dissatisfaction and a surrogate brother as a boyfriend indicatethe complexity of the decisions made to attempt to stabilize her own livelihood in a time of chaos.

Elena's concern for her younger siblings showed a shared responsibility for caring established in the family of origin. This could possibly indicate the value of family (collectivism) before individuality. We are not sure in this situation if her boyfriend is of the same ethnicity, bilingual, or sensitive to Elena's concerns. Her feelings of isolation may be indicative of a grieving process due to her parents' divorce. They might also be attributable to a lack of support in her current environment, a sense of responsibility for her siblings' wellbeing, or feelings of helplessness in her ability to take care of things. Not being able to use he language of emotion, which could be Spanish, might also be an important factor, especially when coupled with her acculturation process in a new environment of work, relationships, and culture.

Other issues to consider may include her phenotypic characteristics in relation to her environment of employment, socioeconomic status, lack of perceived power, gender and Latina competition issues related to her educational status as compared to other Latinos, out-group status, young age, and possible lack of support systems. There are also indicators of wanting a quick solution through medication to relieve her symptoms. Examining the various options according to the information presented, the counselor may begin to engage with Elena in identifying various empowerment strategies. Empowerment strategies should not be considered until the counselor has explored her/his own cultural, racial, gender, and language biases that may exist in relation to the client.

In Elena's situation, the exploration of her current needs and her relationship with her boyfriend may lead to uncovering issues concerning her family of origin. If Spanish is her language of emotion, and even if the counselor is not Spanish-speaking, encouraging her to speak in Spanish would enable Elena to express herself from a position of comfort and security. This is similar to the empty chair technique. Understanding her role in her family of origin and dedication to her younger siblings' welfare could lead to the possibilities of them visiting her, opening up communication by her visiting her family, or establishing a support network with extended family members. Validating her ability to be successful in decision-making skills may create the possibility of encouraging Elena to use these same skills in understanding some of her struggles in the work environment and her relationship with her boyfriend. Due to her ability to be self-sufficient, Elena may want to return to Puerto Rico and seek employment to be near to and part of her family of origin. In addition, it is possible that the boyfriend is both a support and a hindrance. However, a counselor would not encourage a client to eliminate their coping responses without replacing them with healthy ones. Overall, Elena has many skills. She is educated, self-sufficient, intelligent, motivated, and creative. The combination of these factors allows for a variety of empowerment strategies.

Edwin presents a different situation because of his acquired disability. "When an individual suffers some disability or impairment, whether mental or physical, he or she is labeled as such. Unfortunately, such labels often imply dependence and limited worth" (Lewis, Lewis, Daniels & D'Andrea, 1998, p. 173).

Dealing with a disability often creates feelings of grief, frustration, guilt, and anger. The combination of these feelings may result in an internalization of learned helplessness resulting in depression. The acquired disability has forced Edwin, willingly or unwillingly, to redefine his male role and identity in relation to his family and to make adaptations in his cultural perceptions related to machismo and work identity. His relationship with his wife also has been redefined. All of these issues directly relate to his perceived gender role within the nuclear family, as well as to his social isolation, marginal social status, and actual and perceived power related to age and male privilege.

Edwin's reactions to his current situation may indicate that he was a proud provider for the family, ensuring economic support for the family's wellbeing. Many of these roles are traditional male roles defined through Edwin's culture. Superimposing a disability onto Edwin's view of his family roles threatens his identity as a male, husband, and father. What is apparent about Edwin is that he shows caring and a strong sense of responsibility toward his children's welfare. He demonstrated this by making arrangements with a local priest for schooling that benefited his children. Edwin also has a strong work ethic. This is apparent by his desire to return to work. He also believes that he should be a strong and independent husband, as indicated through his withstanding of considerable pain from the work injury without complaining.

Finally, Edwin is able, with *dignidad* and still maintaining *orgullo* (pride), to communicate with others to get some of his family's needs met, as shown with his interaction with the local priest and his willingness to participate in counseling.

Empowerment strategies would of necessity have to consider the situation holistically. The disability is forcing Edwin to reconsider his values and beliefs of himself as a man, husband, and father. His definition of a man has to be reframed and become flexible in order to cognitively assimilate a more androgynous existence in his relationship with others. The acceptance of this definition would provide greater interdependency and power-sharing in the relationship with his wife. In turn, it would lower his threatening view of her success and happiness with her contribution to the family's welfare. The acceptance of the interdependency would help Edwin redefine the importance of his role as a major caretaker for his children. These experiences could strengthen his relationships with his children and expand his sensitivity to child care. While these issues of interdependency are being addressed Edwin could also pursue the possibility of being retrained or reeducated in another field of work that could meet some of his occupational needs. Edwin could also learn about the grieving process related to experiencing a sudden disability. How does a counselor empower Edwin to accomplish these goals?

Apparently, Edwin felt comfortable in consulting with the local priest in addressing some of his family's needs. The counselor may have to serve as a cultural broker in establishing credibility, support, and understanding of Edwin's needs. Edwin has many strengths that were discussed. Capitalizing on his perceptions of strength and engaging an acceptable cultural healer (priest) as part of his treatment could provide the empowerment needed for Edwin to be successful in meeting his and his family's needs.

Francisca's strengths are immediately observable: she is employed, has healthcare insurance, can admit to physical maladies and is willing to seek help. All of these behaviors indicate resourcefulness and personal empowerment. This is not a helpless or passive woman, often the stereotype about Latinas. Furthermore, her purpose for working is tied directly to her son's benefit. Presumably, Francisca took some risks in coming to the United States alone. Again, more characteristically, men are the more typical single immigrants.

A culturally competent counselor would recognize Francisca's need to connect through small talk or *plática*. This is indicative of personalismo and mutuality. The culturally uninformed counselor would likely label this as inappropriate and intrusive behavior, electing not to self-disclose her/his ethnicity and interpret her questions as forms of resistance. To do so would ensure the likelihood that Francisca would not return to counseling. How could she respect someone who is not willing to share about family?

To work from Latino/a perspectives of empowerment, the counselor would have to be willing to engage in reciprocal *plática* and see this form of dialogue as a possible therapeutic process for the client. Additionally, the counselor needs to acknowledge Francisca's strengths and coping mechanisms. Once this stage is set, the counselor can inquire further about the physical symptoms of pains and tiredness. It is important not to jump to conclusions and interpretations about what may appear to be psychosomatic manifestations. Empowerment strategies are about first meeting clients at their base of strength.

Empowerment and Advocacy

Without a doubt, advocacy and empowerment are both very positive terms in the counseling world, but the application of these concepts must occur based on cultural competency. In many ways, advocacy and empowerment are both culturally relative and culturally universal concepts and practices. The counselor must continually make determinations about whether to employ strategies that are culturally relative to the Latino client's situation and environment or whether to apply a practice that one has used successfully with non-Latino clients. How can one predict what will be the most appropriate intervention or technique to use in a particular situation?

The Multicultural Counseling Competencies describe the domain of "culturally appropriate intervention strategies." Inherent in these competencies is the capacity to be culturally aware, knowledgeable and skilled when well-meaning advocacy is intended, particularly in institutional settings. For example, in California and in other states, there have been movements against bilingual education. In a school setting, a counselor may advocate for the immigrant parents who want to see their children in a bilingual education classroom temporarily but who feel pressure from the administration to move the child into an ESL (English as a Second Language) classroom. Culturally appropriate intervention strategies must take into consideration the individual, institutional, and sociopolitical pressure aimed toward the status quo. I may want to strongly encourage ESL because I believe learning English quickly will reduce the child's discriminatory experiences and because the administration will approve of this action, but this action might send a message of cultural insensitivity, not empowerment, to the parents.

One final thought: Sometimes there is a fine line between advocacy and patronizing behavior. Latinos are highly oriented to respect for authority but also have a strong sense of self-determination. In U.S. society, we always have to anticipate the behavior of representatives of the mainstream. With counseling, this anticipation and guardedness also occurs. Observe your own thought process the next time you are in an advocacy situation with Latinos—what is patronizing behavior versus genuine helping?

Conclusion

The operationalized multicultural counseling competencies (1996) specify content areas of awareness, knowledge, and skills that can lead to culturally competent empowerment. The consideration of the Latino cultural values and other variables allows the counselor to begin to develop a framework of counseling based on individual differences and cultural background. Such a framework would consist of the counselor's self-awareness of his or her own personal issues related to worldview, identity, and acculturation. Awareness of worldview would require counselors to examine their assumptions and values about a person's existence in society, within a family, and individually. Identity consists of how counselors have developed their roles as helping professionals and as individuals in interpersonal relationships. This concept also includes the assumptions of the theoretical orientation from which the counselor has chosen to work with the client. The concept of acculturation addresses the degree to which the counselor's assumptions of "normal" behaviors allow for enough flexibility to accept diverse forms of behaviors that the client may present.

The ability of counselors to use empowerment strategies depends on such interacting areas as level of self-awareness, knowledge, and skills; respect for the worldview of Latino clients; ability to view people from a strength rather than a deficit perspective; and willingness to suspend judgment and premature interpretation about the clients' presenting issues. The same qualities must also be present when we use advocacy strategies. Successful advocacy, like successful counseling, requires rapport, unconditional positive regard, and equity, all of which are characteristic of the Latino cultural values and perspectives discussed in this paper. Everyone should learn more about these and other culture-specific frameworks, and put the Multicultural Counseling Competencies (Sue, Arredondo & McDavis, 1992 and Arredondo, Et al., 1996) on the top of one's reading list.

References

Arredondo, P. (1991). Counseling Latinas. In C. Lee & B. Richardson (Eds.), *Strategies and Techniques for Multicultural Counseling*. Alexandria, VA: AACD Press.

Arredondo, P., Toporek, R., Brown, S.P., Jones, J. Locke, D., Sanchez, J., and Stadler, H. (1996). Operationalization of the multicultural counseling competencies. *Journal of Multicultural Counseling and Development, 24*(1), 42-78.

Casas, M., & Vasquez, M. (1996). Counseling the Hispanic: A guiding framework for a diverse population. In Paul B. Pedersen, Juris G. Draguns, Walter J. Lonner, & Joseph E. Trimble, 4th Edition, *Counseling across Cultures* (pp. 146-176). Thousand Oaks California: Sage.

Chacón, M., Cohen, E., Camarena, M, Gonzalez, J., & Strover, S. (1985). *Chicanas in California post-secondary education: A comparative study of barriers to program progress*. Stanford, CA: Center for Chicano Research.

Levy, J. (1974). *The autobiography of Cesar Chavez*. New York, NY.: W.W. Norton & Company.

Lewis, J.A., Lewis, M.D., Daniels, J.A. & D'Andrea, M.J. (1998). *Community counseling*, 2nd ed. Pacific Grove, CA.: Brooks/Cole Publishing Company.

Sue, D.W., Arredondo, P. and McDavis, R.J. (1992). Multicultural counseling competencies and standards: A call to the profession. *Journal of Counseling and Development, 70*, 477-486.

Vázquez, L.A., García-Vázquez, E., Bauman, S.A., & Sierra, A.S. (1997). A preliminary study, phenotype and acculturation: Impact on Mexican American students' interest in community. *Hispanic Journal of Behavioral Science, 19* (3), 377-386

Patricia Arredondo is president of Empowerment Workshops, Inc., in Boston, Mass. Luis Vázquez is an assistant professor at New Mexico State University.

Chapter Six

Multiracial families

By Kelley Kenney

The multiracial population is one of the fastest growing segments of the U.S. population. In discussing the multiracial population it is first important to identify and define the groups that are encompassed under the heading of multiracial. Literature on the topic of multiracialism has included interracial couples, multiracial individuals, and families in which a cross-racial or transracial adoption or foster care arrangement has occurred. The following definitions are provided for clarification of the groups that have been identified.

Definitions

Interracial couples — couples, married or not, involving partners who are each members of a different racial/cultural background.

Multiracial individuals — utilized synonymously with the term biracial, multiracial individuals are those persons whose parents are of two or more different racial/cultural backgrounds.

Cross racial/Transracial adoption — adoption of a child who is of a different racial heritage than the adopting parent or parents.

Cross racial/Transracial foster care arrangement — foster care arrangement for a child who is of a different racial heritage than the individual or individuals who are providing the foster care.

Multiracial families — multiracial families may include families that are composed of interracial couples and their multiracial offspring; single parents with biological offspring who are multiracial and single parents who have gone through a surrogate pregnancy process or artificial insemination process which results in the birth of a multiracial child; families in which a cross racial or transracial adoption or foster care arrangement has occurred, and gay or lesbian couples or single individuals who have adopted transracially, are providing transracial foster care, or have gone through a surrogate pregnancy process or artificial insemination process which results in the birth of a multiracial child.

Between 1960 and 1970, the rate of interracial marriages in the U.S. soared by more than 800 percent. U.S. census data reports that approximately one out of every twenty-five marriages is interracial. Nearly 3 million children in the country are of multiracial backgrounds. These figures do not include the large number of families who have become multiracial as a result of adoption or foster care arrangements. An increasing number of these families have become multiracial as a result of international adoptions.

The increasing multiracialization of our society has made for considerable controversy. Myths about mixed marriages, biracial people, and cross-racial adoption emerge from decades of politically and socially constructed racism. This racism not only impacts on our views of multiracial individuals and families, but also influences the level and quality of services available to them. Despite their increasing numbers, very little has been done to encourage an increase in the information and knowledge made available to human service professionals and educators who may be working with the multiracial population. Historically, discussions of ethnicity and culture have focused on persons who identify with one ethnic or cultural group. Hence, we have continued to scrutinize the lives of couples, individuals, and families who are identified as multiracial based upon myths, stereotypes, and other forms of information for which there is no empirical validity.

In working with the multiracial population, we are challenged to examine and address the deeply ingrained oppressive context by which we have viewed people of different ethnicities and cultures. Hence, advocacy with this population begins when we allow ourselves to explore honestly the meaning that our society has attributed to the notion of race, and examine openly what this notion has come to mean to us individually.

Professionals in the counseling, human services, and educational fields are called upon to be multiculturally competent. This competency requires us to function as advocates and social change agents as we carry out the traditional roles and responsibilities of our jobs.

Advocacy and social change for the multiracial population requires counseling, human service, and education professionals to take lead roles in enhancing the knowledge and awareness of persons with whom they work on the characteristics, issues, and concerns of the multiracial population. This is done by first exploring informational resources that may be available about this population. Available resources must be made accessible to schools, churches, and community agencies and must also be made accessible to students of the counseling, human service, and education fields, who will find themselves working more consistently with this population as we move into the new millennium.

Having noticed the dearth of information on this population, people who are part of multiracial families, are multiracial themselves, or have an interest in the topic because of experiences they have had with this population, have begun to add to the professional literature on this topic. For example, Maria Root, a clinical psychologist and fellow of the American Psychological Association who identifies as multiracial, has published numerous professional articles and books regarding the experiences of multiracial individuals. In addition, Lise Funderburg wrote a book which was based both on her own experience as a multiracial individual and on the experiences of 65 other multiracial individuals. Walt Harrington and Mark and Gail Mathabane have written books concerning interracial couples that are based upon their own experiences as partners in interracial marriages. Another form of advocacy for this population involves encouraging and supporting a broader commitment to research and to sound empirical investigation on topics of relevance to the multiracial population, as a way of helping professionals better understand the lives, experiences, and challenges of members of this population. Advocacy also means taking the lead in the development and implementation of school curriculums and training programs that are inclusive of this population and the riches they have to offer.

Across the country, support groups and forums have been developed to provide support and affirmation to members of this population and their families. The existence of these groups have at times provided indications as to whether or not particular parts of the country are welcoming, supportive, or even safe for multiracial individuals and families. Taking this into account, another form of advocacy may involve the development and implementation of support networks in areas where the resources provided by a network would be beneficial to individuals and families. The worldwide web also has an array of resources and networks available for information and support of the multiracial population. Hence, professionals who are advocating for this population need to avail themselves of this information so that they can refer to it, as well as provide it to their constituents and clients as an additional resource option.

The identification of "multiracial" has come under considerable social, political, and economic scrutiny. The multiracial community has challenged the underlying power issues related to this scrutiny by starting a movement to force the federal government to consider the institution of a "multiracial category" on census forms for the year 2000. This movement has also been lobbying for all other government agencies and affiliates to include a multiracial category on forms and reportive documents. In 1997, the decision that was passed down from the U.S. Office of Budget and Management provided a compromise, which will allow individuals to select as many categories that apply to them as they wish.

Identity has been found to greatly impact human development and particularly, the development of self-esteem. If as counselors, human service providers, and educators, we are concerned about assisting in the positive identity development of our constituents, then it makes sense that we need to take a stand toward assisting individuals in achieving an identity that affirms who they are and allows them to feel good about themselves. For the multiracial population, this requires involvement on a political level. Hence, as advocates for this population we need to challenge the political forces within our communities that invalidate the role identifying oneself as multiracial has had upon the self-concepts of those with whom we work. In this regard, our work with school districts, social, civic, and government agencies becomes crucial.

Another very important aspect of advocacy involves going the extra mile for constituents and clients by intervening in ways that can have an impact on a broader, systemic level. For counselors and other human service professionals, this means that while continuing to maintain professionally ethical behavior and judgement, we take on less therapeutically oriented roles with clients. These roles may entail being more involved with our clients in personal, social, and political venues, particularly those that are geared toward increasing societal awareness, acceptance, and affirmation of multiracial individuals and families.

As the multiracial population continues to grow, it is clear that counseling professionals, human service providers, and educators will find themselves working with increasing numbers of this population. As advocates we need to promote awareness and interest in the needs and strengths of the multiracial population and in doing so, insure that the services delivered to this population are done effectively, competently, and respectfully.

A relatively exhaustive list of references is included. In

addition, information from the Internet about support groups that are available across the country and a list of Internet websites offering support and addressing issues of relevance to the multiracial population are also included.

References Related to Multiracial Individuals

Anderson, K. S. (1993). *Ethnic identity in biracial Asian Americans.* Location: University of California, Santa Barbara. Call no.: BF80.7.U62 L7 ANDK 1993a Asian-American Studies.

Atkins, E. (1991, June 5). For many mixed race Americans, life isn't simply black or white. *New York Times*, p. B8.

Atkins, E. (1992, Jan/Feb). Reading, 'riting and race relations. *New People*, 10-11.

Brown, Y. A., & Montague, A. (1992, February 7). Choosing sides. *New Statesman and Society*, 14-15.

Brun, U.M. (1995). Black/white interracial young adults: quests for a racial identity. *American Journal of Orthopsvchiatry, 65*, 125-130.

Butler, P. (1989, November). My white father. *Harper's Magazine*, 36-40.

Camper, C. (Ed.). *Miscegenation blues: Voices of mixed race women.* Canada: Sister Vision, Black Women, and Women of Colour Press.

Courtney, B. A. (1995, February 13). Freedom from choice: Being biracial has meant denying half my identity. *Newsweek*, 16.

French, M. (1994, February 7). Subtle shades of the rainbow. *The Washington Post*, p. Cl (col. 3).

Funderburg, L. (1994). *Black, white, other: Biracial Americans talk about race and identity.* New York: William Morrow and Company, Inc.

Haizlip, S. T. (1995, March). Passing. *American Heritage*, 46.

Johnson, D. J. (1992). Racial preference and biculturality in biracial preschoolers. *Merrill Palmer Ouarterly, 38*, 233-244.

Kitahara, G. (1982). *Eurasians, ethnic/racial identity development of biracial Japanese/white adults.*California State University, Graduate School of Psychology.

Koeppel, L. B. (1987). *The development of the self-concept in biracial offspring of Asian-caucasian intermarriages.* Location: California State University, Northridge.

Lewis, D. (1978). *Mirror reflections of blackness: Identity and biracial children.* Professional Project: George Williams College.

Mahdesran, L. (1987, November). It's not easy being green: On the difficulties of being multiracial. *U.S. News & World Report,* 8.

Minebrook, J. L. (1990, December 24). The pain of a divided family. *U.S. News & World Report,* 40.

Mitchell, J. L. (1991, September 1). Back in the USA. *Los Angeles Times,* p. Jl.

Multi-racial multi-cultural group builds bridges across racial lines. (1992, November). Affirmative: University of Michigan.

Murphy, S. L. H. (1987). *The voices of Amerasians: Ethnicity, identity, and empowerment in interracial Japanese Americans.* Dissertation: Harvard University. Call no. E184 A5 M87.

Nash, R. D. (1995). *Coping as a biracial/biethnic teen.* New York: Rosen Publishing Group.

Njeri, I. (1991, September). Who is black? *Essence,* 64-66.

Pagnozzi, A. (1991, September). Mixing it up. *Mirabella,* 130-132.

Poe, J. (1992, May 3). Multiracial people want a single name that fits. *Chicago Tribune,* p. Al+.

Rebirth of a nation. (1993, Fall). *Time* (Special Issue), 66-67.

Reddy, M. T. (1994). *Crossing the color line: race, parenting, and culture.* New Brunswick, NJ: Rutgers University Press.

Root, M. P. P. (1992). *Racially mixed people in America.* Newburg Park, CA: Sage Publications.

Root, M. P. P. (1996). *The multiracial experience*. Thousand Oaks, CA: Sage Publications.

Rutherford, D. (1990). *Writing a book for young children focusing on biracial Chinese American children, families and lifestyles*. Location: Pacific Oaks College.

Saenz, R., Haking, S., & Aguime, B. E. (1995). Persistence and change in Asian identity among children of intermarried couples. *Sociological Perspective, 38*, 175-194.

Sandor, G. (1994, June). The 'other' Americans. *American Demographics*, 36.

Santiago, R. (1989, November). Black and Latino. *Essence*, 12.

Scales-Trent, J. (1990, Spring). Commonalities: On being black and white, different and the same. *Yale Journal of Law and Feminism*, 305-327.

Shanker, W. (1989, September 20). New group discusses multi-racial issues. *Michigan Daily*, p. 3.

Wijeyesinghe, C. (1992). *Towards an understanding of the racial identity of bi-racial people: The experience of racial self-identification of African-American/Euro-American adults and the factors affecting their choices of racial identity*. Location: University of California, Santa Barbara. Call no.: LB 1715.M4 A 37 WL~C 1992a.

Williams, G. H. (1995). *Life of the color line*. New York: Plume/Penguin.

McBride, J. (1996). *The color of water: A black man's tribute to his white mother*. New York: Riverhead Books.

Zack,N. (Ed.). (1995). *American mixed race: The culture of microdiversity*. Lanham, MD: Rowman & Littlefield Publishers.

Periodicals Dedicated to Interracial Issues

AMEA Networking News. c/o Connie Hannah 833 Mt. Pleasant RD. Chesapeake, VA 23320.

Interrace Magazine. PO Box 12048 Atlanta, GA 30355. 404-358-7877. A magazine for teens and adults involved in interracial relationships. Biracial Child is geared for kids 5-12 years old.

Interrace: The Source for Interracial Living. PO Box 15566 Beverly Hills, CA 90209.

Interracial Classified. PO Box 185 College Point, NY 11356-0185.

Interracial Club of Buffalo Newsletter. PO Box 400 Amherst Branch, Buffalo, NY 14226.

I-Pride: Interracial, Intercultural Pride. PO Box 191752, San Francisco, CA 94119-1752. Published by support group for multiracial people. Events and articles.

New People: The Journal for the Human Race. PO Box 47490 Oak Park, MI 48237.

Society for Interracial Families Newsletter. 23399 Evergreen, Suite 2222 Southfield, MI 48075.

Teaching Intolerance Magazine. Southern Poverty Law Center. 400 Washington Ave., Montgomery, AL 36104. FAX: 205-264-3121.

Catalogs of Books/Supplies with Multiracial/Ethnic/Cultural Themes

Arte Publico Press. Issues regular press releases of books with Hispanic themes. University of Houston. Houston, TX 77204-2090. 713-743-2999.

Council on Interracial Books for Children. Send SASE for a list of resources. 1841 Broadway, New York, NY 10023.

Great Owl Books. "A unique collection of children' s books celebrating the many voices of our American culture. Ask about our special catalog for biracial children, adults and families !" Margot Sage-El, c/o Great Owl Books 41 Watchung Plaza, Suite 112 Montclair, NJ 07042. 1-800-299-3181. FAX: 1-201-783-5899.

Highsmith Multicultural Bookstore. Authentic Multicultural Books and Media. Highsmith, Inc. W5227 Highway 106, PO Box 800 Fort Atkinson, WI 53538-0800. 1-800-558-2110.

InterSpectrum. A mail order catalog featuring merchandise for the interracial community.

Sandy & Son Educational Supplies. Write or call for free catalog of wooden puzzles of interracial families. 215 Hampshire Street Inman Square Cambridge, MA 02139. 617-491-6290.

Savanna Books. Send for complete catalog. 72 Chestnut Street Cambridge, MA 02139. 617-876-7665.

Seal Press. 3131 Western Avenue, Suite 410 Seattle, WA 98121©1041. 206-283-7844. FAX: 206-285-9410. E-mail: sealprss @ scn.org.

Tapestry Books. Publishers of the Adoption Book Catalog. PO Box 359 Ringoes, NJ 08551. 908-806-6695. FAX: 908-788-2999.

Counseling Multiracial Individuals and Families
SelectedReferences on Biracial Identity

Adoff, A. (1982). *All the colors of the race.* New York: Lothrop, Lee, & Shepard Books. [poetry from children's perspective]

Anderson, K. S. (1994). Ethnic identity in biracial Asian Americans. *Dissertation Abstracts International, 54* (9-B), 4905.

Brown, P. M. (1990). Biracial identity and social marginality. *Child & Adolescent Social Work Journal, 7,* 319-337.

Chin, J. L., Liem, J. H., Ham, M. D. C., & Hong, G. K. (1993). *Transference and empathy in American psychotherapy: Cultural values and treatment needs.* Westport, CT: Praeger Pub/Greenwood Pub.

Gibbs, J. T. (1991). Biracial adolescents. In J. T. Gibbs & L. N. Huang (Eds.), *Children of color: Psychological interventions with minority youth* (pp. 322-350). San Francisco: Jossey Bass.

Hall, C. I. (1997). Best of both worlds: Body image and satisfaction of a sample of Black-Japanese biracial individuals. In V. H. Houston & T. K. Williams (Eds.), *No passing zone: The artistic and discursive voices of Asian-descent multiracials.* Amerasia Journal, 23 (1), 87-97.

Herring, R. D. (1995). Developing biracial ethnic identity: A review of the increasing dilemma. *Journal of Multicultural Counseling and Development, 23,* 29-38.

Hershel, H. J. (1995). Therapeutic perspectives on biracial identity formation and internalized oppression. In N. Zach (Ed.), *American mixed race: The culture of microdiversity* (pp. 169-181). Lanham MD: Rowman & Littlefield.

Kerwin, C. & Ponterotto, J. G. (1995). Biracial identity development: Theory and research. In J.G. Ponterotto, J. M. Casas, L. A. Suzuki, & C. M. Alexander (Eds.), *Handbook of Multicultural Counseling* (199-217). Thousand Oaks CA: Sage Pub.

McBride, J. (1996). *The color of water a Black man's tribute to his white mother.* New York: Riverhead Books.

Miller, R. L. & Miller, B. (1990). Mothering the biracial child: Bridging the gaps between African American and White parenting styles. Special issue: Motherhood: A feminist perspective. *Women & Therapy, 10,* 169-179.

Moraga, C. (1994). *From a long line of Vendidas: Chicanas and feminism.* Boulder CO: Westview Press.

Nishimura, N. J. (1995). Addressing the needs of biracial children: An issue for counselors in a multicultural school environment. *School Counselor, 43,* 52-57.

Pinderhughes, E. (1995). Biracial identity—asset or handicap? In H.W. Harris, H. C. Blue, & E. E. H. Griffin (Eds.), *Racial and ethnic identity: Psychological development and creative expression* (pp. 73-93). NewYork: Routledge.

Poston, W. C. (1990). The biracial identity development model: A needed addition. *Journal of Counseling and Development, 69,* 152-155.

Root, M. P. P. (Ed.). (1992). *Racially mixed people in America.* Thousand Oaks CA: Sage Pub.

Root, M. P. P. (1995). Resolving "other status: Identity development of biracial individuals. In N. R. Goldberger & J. B. Veroff (Eds.), *The culture and psychology reader.* New York: New York University Press.

Root, M. P. P. (Ed.). (1996). *The multiracial experience: Racial borders as the new frontier.* Thousand Oaks CA: Sage Pub.

Thrasher, S. M. (1994). Well-being in a biracial sample: Racial identification and similarity to parents. *Dissertation Abstracts International, 54* (8-B), 4411.

Winn, N. N. & Priest, R. (1993). Counseling biracial children: A forgotten component of multicultural counseling. *Family Therapy*, *20*, 29-36.

Websites

- Hapa Issues Forum Home Page: llwww. wenet . net/~hapa/

- Interrace Haven: www.eden.com/~crusader/irhaven.html/

- Interracial/Biracial Resource List: www.lclark.edu/~absher/biracial.html/

- *My Shoes* support group for biracial/multiracial persons who have a white appearance: myshoes. com

- Biliography Resources by and about Interracial and Multicultural People: www.personal.umich.edu/~kdown/multi.html

Books for Children

Africa Dream by Eloise Greenfield
Kids Explore America's Hispanic Heritage by Westridge Young Writers Workshop
Hopscotch Around the World by Mark Lankford
Free to be a Family by Marlo Thomas— cassette and book
Growing Up Adopted by Maxine Rosenberg
Being Adopted by Maxine Rosenberg
Families are Different by Nina Pellegrini
A Family for Jamie by Suzanne Bloom
Horace by Holly Keller
How it Feels to be Adopted by Jill Krementz
Katie-Bo: An Adoption Story by Iris L. Fisher
Lucy' s Feet by Stephanie Stein
A Mother for Choco by Keiko Kasza
The Mulberry Bird by Ann Braff Brodzinsky
Real for Sure Sister by Ann Angel
Susan and Gordon Adopt a Baby by Judy Freudberg and Tony Geiss
Through Moon and Stars and Night Skies by Ann Turner
We Adopted You Benjamin Koo by Bobbie Jane Kates (Sesame St. book)

Why am I Different? by Norma Simon
On the Day You Were Born by Debra Frazier
Starry Night by David Spohn
Winter Wood by David Spohn
Living in Two Worlds by Maxine Rosenberg
One World One Child - photo book
People by Peter Spier
The People Atlas by Philip Steele
We're Different We're the Same by Bobbie Jane Kates (Sesame St. book)
Amazing Grace by Mary Hoffman
All the Colors of the Race by Arnold Adoff
Cornrows by Camille Yarbrough
Honey I Love by Eloise Greenfield
Jambo Means Hello: Swahili Alphabet Book by Muriel and Tom Feelings
Moha Means One: Swahili Counting Book by Muriel and Tom Feelings
The People Could Fly-American Black Folktales by Virginia Hamilton
The Adventures of Connie and Diego by Maria Garcia
The Grandchildren of the Incas by Matti Pitkanen
Ten Little Rabbits by Virginia Grossman and Sylvia Long
Why There is No Arguing in Heaven by Deborah Nourse Lattimore
Black is Brown is Tan by Arnold Adoff
Mama Do You Love Me? by Barbara Joosse
Baby-O by Nancy White Carlstrom
Abuela by Arthur Dorros

References Related to Multiracial Children and Adolescents

Albrecht, B. E. (1993, April 11). Being biracial: It's no big deal to children of mixed colors. *The Plain Dealer*, p. 1G+.

Are the children of mixed marriages black or white? (1990, May 21). *Jet*, 52-54.

Barringer, F. (1989, September 24). Mixed race generation emerges but is not sure where it fits. *New York Times, section 1*, p. 22.

Bowles, D. D. (1993, Winter). Bi-racial identity: Children born to African-American and white couples. *Clinical Social Work Journal.*

Brown, U. M. (1995, January). Black/white interracial young adults: Quest for a racial identity. *American Journal of Orthopsvchiatrv*, 125.

Buttery, T. (1987, May). Helping interracial children adjust. *Biracial Children*, 38-41.

Campbell, P. Conference addresses needs of interracial children. *Interracial Books for Children Bulletin*, *15* (5), 13-14.

Charles, N. (1991, April 26). A special blend of American folks. *The Plain Dealer* (Cleveland, OH), p. E-1+.

Capan, M., & Suarez, C. (1993, June). Biracial/biethnic characters in young adult and children's books. *Multicultural Review*, 32-37.

Collins, J., & David, R. J. (1993, August). Race and birthweight in biracial infants. *American Journal of Public Health*, 1125-1129.

Crispell, D. (1993, January 27). Interracial children pose challenge for classifiers. *The Wall Street Journal*, p. B 1 (W), p. B 1 (E).

Folaron, G., & Hess, P. M. (1993, March-April). Placement considerations for children of mixed African American and caucasian parentage. *Child Welfare*, 113-125.

Forna, A. (1988, December). A racial caste-away? *British Cosmopolitan*, 71.

Gibbs, J. T., & Moskowitz-Sweet, G. (1991, December). Clinical and cultural issues in the treatment of biracial and bicultural adolescents. *Families in Society*, 579-592.

Gonzalez, D. (1992, November 17). For Afro-Amerasians, tangled emotions surface. *The New York Times*, p. C19 (N).

Herring, A. (1995). Developing biracial ethnic identity: A review of the increasing dilemma. *Journal of Multicultural Counseling and Development*, *23*, 29-38.

Herring, R. D. (1992, December). Biracial children: An increasing concern for elementary and middle school counselors. *Elementary School Guidance and Counseling*, 123-130.

Interracial baby boom. (1993, May©June). *The Futurist*, 54-55.

Johnson, R. C., & Nagoshi, C. (1986, May). The adjustment of offspring of within group and interracial/intercultural marriages: A comparison of personality factor scores. *Journal ofMarriage and Family*, 279-284.

Kalish, S. (1995). Multiracial births increase as US ponders racial definitions. *Population Today, 23* (4), 1-2.

Ladner, J. Providing a healthy environment for interracial children. *Interracial Books for Children Bulletin, 15* (6), 7-8.

Lawren, B. (1985, February). Interracial kids. *Omni*, 36.

Leslie, C. (1995, February 13). The loving generation. *Newsweek*, 125, 72.

McNamee, M. (1994, July 4). Should the census be less black and white? *Business Week*, 40.

Mura, D. (1992, September-October). What should I tell Samantha, my biracial daughter, about secrets and anger? *Mother Jones*, 18-21.

No place for mankind. (1989, September 4). *Time*, 17.

Norment, L. (1985, September). A probing look at children of interracial marriages. *Ebony*, 156-162.

Oriti, B., Bibb, A., & Mahbabi, J. (1996). Family-centered practice with racially-ethnically mixed families. *Families in Society, 77* (9), 573-582.

Parker, L. B. (1992, September-October). My dad is black, my mom is white. *The Black Collegian.* 48-5 1.

Phinney, J. S., & Alipuria, L. L. (1996). *At the interface of cultures*:

Multiethnic/multiracial high school and college students. *The Journal of Social Psychology. 136*, 139-158.

Ponterotto, J. G., Jackson, B. L., & Kerwin, C. (1993, April). Racial identity in biracial children: A qualitative investigation. *Journal of Counseling Psychologv*, 221-231.

Poston, W. S. C. (1990, November-December). The biracial identity development model: A needed addition. *Journal of Counseling and Development*, 152-155.

Reid, T. R. (1993, November 21). U.S.-Japan custody fights gets bitter. *The Washington Post*, p. A32.

Richardson, B. L. (1992, August). Not all black and white. *Glamour*, 252.

Roberts, M. (1987, April). Mixed but equal. *Psychology Today*, 18.

Rosin, H. (1994, January 4). Boxed in. *The New Republic*, 12.

Stevens, R. (1989, April 7). Growing up beige. *Scholastic Update* (teachers edition), p.9.

Thomas, D. (1993). Black, white, or other? *Essence*, 24, 118.

Updike, D. (1992, January). The colorings of childhood. *Harper's Magazine*, 63-66+.

Updike, D. (1994, July 31). Coloring lessons. *The New York Times Magazine*, p. 14.

Udansky, M. L. (1992, December 11). For interracial kids, growth spurt. *USA Today*, p. A-1+.

War's postscript (Vietnamese children of American GI's want to leave Vietnam). (1988, July). *Life*, 38.

Wardle, F. (1987, January). Are you sensitive to interracial children's special needs? *Young Children*, 53-59.

Wardle, F. (1991, Winter). Raising interracial children. *Mothering*, 111-117.

Whitaker, C. (1992, October). The true story of an Indiana 'white' boy who discovered that he was black. *Ebony*, 115.

Willerman, L. (1970, December). Intellectual development of children from interracial matings. *Science*, 1329-1331.

Williams, O. B. (1992, June 14). I just don't understand you (in black and white). *Detroit News*.

Winn, N. N., & Priest, R. (1993). Counseling biracial children: A forgotten component of multicultural counseling. *Family Therapy*, 20 (1), 29-36.

Wrights, B. J. (1984, December). Can Santa be black? *Ms.*, 121-122.

World trends and forecasts: Demographics: Interracial baby boom. (1993, May-June). *Futurist*, 54-55.

Yudkin, M. (1991, October 20). Chen's mother. *The New York Times Magazine*, p 22+.

Kelley Kenney is a professor of counselor education at Kutztown University in Kutztown, Penn.

Chapter Seven

Youth advocacy

Michael D'Andrea and Judy Daniels

According to the American Heritage Desk Dictionary (1981) the term "advocate" is defined in the following way: "A person who argues for a cause; a supporter or defender" (p. 16). Using this definition as a guide, it is logical to think of a "youth advocate" as a person who argues for, supports and defends the rights of youths. It is interesting to note that, while many counselors provide advocacy services to promote the psychological health and personal well-being of youngsters and adolescents, they do not always view themselves as "youth advocates." This is due, in part, to the fact that few publications have directed attention to the counselor's role as a youth advocate in the professional counseling literature. Because little has been written about advocacy services, many counselors are not aware of the ways in which they are currently acting as advocates or the things they could do to advocate for the rights of their young clients in the future.

What do We Mean by Advocacy?

Recognizing the need to promote a clearer understanding of what the term "advocacy" means and how it can be used in counseling practice, we have taken time in this article to examine this important though often underutilized intervention strategy. In thinking about ways in which they can use advocacy services in their work, we have noted that counselors should begin advocacy efforts by "identifying groups of people who might benefit from increasing their own strength" (Lewis, Lewis, Daniels, & D'Andrea, 1998, p. 25). This includes those groups of persons whose personal needs and concerns are not supported or respected by individuals who have the power to establish rules, policies, and/or laws that affect their lives.

There are literally millions of people in our society who are not given the opportunity to participate fully in establishing rules, policies, and/or laws that affect their lives. These groups of people have been referred to as "socially devalued populations" (Lewis et al., 1998). Socially devalued populations include but are not limited to poor people, gay and lesbian persons, elderly individuals, persons who are physically challenged, culturally and racially diverse individuals, and youths, to name a few. These individuals are often subjected to various forms of prejudice, discrimination, and negative stereotyping that result in their being misunderstood, separated from, and stigmatized by the mainstream community. Because individuals in these socially devalued groups typically have limited power and little say about things that happen in their families, schools, workplaces, and/or communities, they frequently come to believe that they are not valued by others. When a person's sense of self-worth and personal power is eroded, individuals commonly exhibit various types of antisocial behaviors and/or mental health problems.

Because so many people experience a sense of powerlessness in their lives, counselors should go beyond the use of traditional counseling services (e.g., the use of individual, intrapsychic-focused therapeutic approaches). We have to implement advocacy services that are intentionally aimed at helping people acquire a greater sense of self-worth and collective empowerment in their lives. In discussing the importance of using advocacy services in counseling practice, McWhirter (1994) notes that such services should be intentionally designed to: (a) increase the healthy psychological functioning of individuals in socially devalued populations and (b) promote the collective empowerment of those socially devalued populations of which their clients are a part.

Although counselors are professionally and ethically responsible for advocating for the rights and mental health of all socially devalued persons, they really need to pay special attention to the importance of using advocacy services when working with young people. It is particularly important to advocate for the rights and psychological well-being of young people because their sense of self-worth and personal power is often undermined by disempowering policies, practices, and institutions in society. Because this article is specifically written for counseling practitioners who work with youths, we provide a concrete example of the type of advocacy that fostered the empowerment of adolescents. The Nashville Youth Network (NYN) was intentionally designed to assist youths in developing a broad range of skills that they could use to address situations that might otherwise have been disempowering.

The Nashville Youth Network (NYN): An Example of Youth Advocacy

NYN is an alternative youth service project that was designed to promote adolescent development by encouraging teenagers to constructively address concerns and problems they were encountering in their lives. Besides directing their attention to many of the problems adults commonly associate with the teenage years (e.g., drug and alcohol misuse/abuse, school dropouts, teen pregnancies, etc.), the young people who participated in this program also expressed interest in dealing with other types of problems that frequently receive much less attention by youth service providers. This included the lack of respect they felt from many adults, the lack of "real" input they had regarding unfair school policies and practices, and the failure of government officials and other community policy-makers to solicit feedback from adolescents when developing of laws and policies that had a direct impact on the lives of young people.

Individual Youth Advocacy Services

The Nashville Youth Network (NYN) scheduled their weekly meetings at one of the local high schools. Between 15 to 50 adolescents regularly attended these meetings. The teenagers who participated in this organization identified an adult adviser (one of the authors of this article) who they both trusted and viewed as being potentially helpful when discussing possible ways of addressing the various problems and concerns that were raised during the NYN meetings. As a result, the adult adviser played an important role in this organization by: (1) providing information about youth service agencies and other types of resources that were available in the community, (2) supporting the youths as they discussed various problems and concerns they experienced in their lives, and (3) encouraging them as they developed strategies to effectively deal with these problems and concerns.

Besides benefiting from her role as a "program consultant," numerous teenagers in NYN also talked to the adult adviser about personal concerns and/or problems they were encountering in their own lives. However, rather than establishing a formal counseling relationship with these individuals, the adviser maintained her role as consultant and:

(a) carefully listened to the various issues/problems that the teenagers described to her (which typically involved issues related to alcohol/drug use, sexuality, and family problems);

(b) communicated a genuine sense of concern about the personal problems the youths were experiencing;

(c) collected information about the specific concerns that the teenagers expressed; and

(d) referred the teenagers to appropriate youth service providers who were trained in the specific area in which the teenagers were experiencing problems.

Many of the youths who spoke to the adult adviser about their personal concerns were initially resistant to the notion of voluntarily seeking counseling services for their problems. However, by explaining the benefits that can be derived from counseling and emphasizing issues of confidentiality which counselors are bound, many of the teenagers in NYN voluntarily sought professional counseling services to help them deal with serious problems they were experiencing. By taking the time to respectfully advocate for the use of these sort of counseling services, the adult adviser was able to assist individual youths (who were initially very resistant to the idea) to voluntarily participate in programs and services that were designed to foster their psychological health and sense of personal well-being.

Small Group Youth Advocacy Interventions

Many of the teenagers who participated in NYN expressed concern about the drug and alcohol-related problems that some of their friends were experiencing. These youths were particularly frustrated that the public schools were not doing enough to educate youngsters about the problems that are commonly associated with alcohol and drug abuse. As a result of discussing this issue during NYN meetings, the adolescents agreed that more time, energy and resources should be directed towards providing preventive alcohol and drug education services to younger children as a way of dealing with the problem of adolescent substance abuse.

Consequently, the youths asked the adult adviser for assistance in developing strategies and skills they needed to implement a preventive intervention in the elementary schools in the area. The adult advisor and the adolescents in NYN proceeded to work together to develop a "puppet show" that focused on the harmful effects that drinking and drugs can have on different parts of the body. After the puppet show was organized, the adult adviser helped the teenagers develop "marketing strategies" which were designed to let elementary school principals and counselors know about this innovative preventive education service. As a result of their efforts, the alcohol and drug prevention puppet show became a very popular youth advocacy project in the community. By presenting the puppet show to hundreds of elementary school-aged students over the course of several years, the teenagers in NYN gained a greater sense of collective empowerment as they helped youngsters gain a better understanding of the importance of developing healthy lifestyles and avoid making life choices that would negatively impact their lives in the future.

Organizational Advocacy

Besides implementing these alcohol and drug prevention advocacy services in the elementary schools, the teenagers in NYN were also interested in promoting organizational changes in their own high schools. They hoped that such changes would lead school personnel to: (a) gain greater understanding of their needs and concerns and (b) encourage them to treat teenagers in more sensitive, respectful, and supportive ways. With these goals in mind, the NYN members worked with the adult adviser to plan strategies for promoting constructive organizational changes in their schools.

By helping the youths in NYN to: (1) develop a plan which was aimed at promoting positive changes at their schools, (2) acquire the types of consultation skills they would need to effectively implement their organizational development strategies, and (3) providing constant support and encouragement for their efforts, the adult adviser was able to play an important "behind the scenes role" in advocating for the rights and well-being of these youths. These efforts resulted in several NYN representatives meeting with school administrators and members of the local school board to: (a) discuss ways in which out-dated school policies could be altered to more effectively address the needs and concerns of contemporary youths, (b) provide examples of new policies that reflect greater understanding and respect for the psychological needs of youths, and (c) advocate for youth representation on the local school board.

Systemic Youth Advocacy Services

Because they were interested in extending their advocacy efforts beyond the sort of organizational change strategies that were discussed above, the adolescents in NYN began to discuss ways in which they might have an even more profound and lasting impact on the lives of adolescents in the community. When the adult adviser was asked for advice in this area, she helped the teenagers gain a better understanding of the importance of promoting systemic changes in the institutions that create policies and allocate resources that effect schools and other organizations in their community. By helping these teenagers acquire a basic understanding of systems theory, the adult adviser fostered an increased sense of personal empowerment as the adolescents in NYN began talking about ways in which they could work to create longer lasting systemic changes in their community.

This sense of increased collective empowerment led to discussions about ways in which they could work with local and state elected officials to influence future legislative actions that were related to youth issues. By advocating for the development and implementation of systemic change strategies, the adult adviser offered her support, encouragement, and technical assistance by:

(1) consulting with the teenagers about ways in which they could gain the support of elected officials regarding the importance of drafting legislation that reflected greater sensitivity, understanding, and respect for the needs of youths in the state;

(2) helping representatives from NYN set up a series of meetings with elected officials that focused on a broad range of youth-related issues; and

(3) working with the teenagers in NYN as they convened a state-wide "Youth Constitutional Convention." This Youth Constitutional Convention was designed to bring teenagers together from across the state to discuss ways in which the state constitution could be amended so that the rights of children and youth would be better guaranteed in their schools and communities.

Conclusion

Because youths often lack the knowledge and skills to constructively address the problems and challenges they encounter in their lives, they often make choices that result in negative outcomes. The various individual, small group, organizational, and systemic youth advocacy services that are described in this article provide counselors with new ways of thinking about the role they can play in promoting the psychological health and personal well-being of larger numbers of youths in the future. The advocacy services that were outlined above represent only a few of the many ways in which counselors can help foster healthy adolescent development by moving beyond the sort of individual crisis counseling services that many practitioners overutilize in their work.

References

American Heritage Desk Dictionary (1981). New York: Houghton-Mifflin.

Lewis, J. A., Lewis, M. D., Daniels, J., & D'Andrea, M. (1998). *Community counseling: Empowerment strategies for a diverse society.* Pacific Grove, CA: Brooks/Cole.

McWhirter, E. H. (1994). *Counseling for empowerment.* Alexandria, VA: American Counseling Association.

Michael D'Andrea and Judy Daniels are both professors in the department of counselor education at the University of Hawaii in Manoa.

Chapter Eight

Advocating on Behalf of Older Adults

Jane Goodman & Elinor Waters

"Baby Boomers Turning 50"
"Can We Really Afford Social Security?"
"77 Year Old Returns to Space"

The popular press as well as professional journals bombard us with headlines like the above. Clearly, a major demographic trend in the United States today is the aging of the population.

Approximately 34 million people—13 percent of the population of the United States—are 65 or older. That number is expected to more than double to 70 million by 2030 when they will constitute 20 percent of the population. The older population is primarily female and the disparity increases with age. There are 145 women for every 100 men over 65, and 257 women for every 100 men over 85. It is the over 85 group which is the fastest growing segment of the U.S. population and a major reason we need to pay more attention to long-term care.

Our aging population necessitates some new ways of thinking about what it means to be old, and even what "old" is. According to the Department of Labor, older workers are those over 40. Individuals are invited to join the American Association of Retired Persons (AARP) at age 50, and are eligible for senior discounts at different ages. Traditionally, people 65 and over have been considered "old," and that has been the age at which Americans have been eligible for full social security benefits. But that, too, is changing.

Stereotypes abound. Some people think of older adults as being uneducated and impoverished, while others see them as "greedy geezers." The reality is that older adults are probably more varied than other age cohorts as they have had more years to develop their differences. They run the gamut from frisky to frail, from wealthy to poor, and from socially active to isolated.

Many older adults have serious mental health problems, with depression being the most common. Estimates are that nearly 15 percent of community living older adults and at least 25 percent of nursing home residents suffer from depression. Other problems include anxiety disorders, substance abuse, and cognitive impairment. Unfortunately, many of these mental health needs are unmet. This stems, in part, from the reluctance of many in this age cohort to seek mental health assistance. We may need to encourage Mental Health Workers to provide more informal "consultation" or "by-the-way counseling" to people reluctant to seek formal mental health services. Other factors include: the scarcity of both community-based preventive programs and institutionally based treatment programs; the fact that health insurance plans typically give short shrift to mental health benefits; and the lack of coordination between the aging network, the mental health network, and the primary care delivery system.

Why Advocacy?

It is not just the increasing numbers that make it important for us to serve as advocates for this group. All of us are in some way connected to older adults. We may be older ourselves. If not, we certainly hope to acquire that status! Ageism may be one form of discrimination that all of us who live long enough may encounter. Older adults, particularly women, are often marginalized by society, sometimes patronized, and other times ignored. Many are vulnerable as they are unschooled in dealing with bureaucracies, or inhibited by authorities. Elder abuse is a growing problem, often triggered when families are stressed beyond their coping capacities.

On the positive side there is evidence that advocacy works. Mandatory retirement has been eliminated, giving those who wish to work after 65 that opportunity. And Social Security now pays benefits not only to wives and widows, but also to divorced women who were married for 10 or more years.

While all these factors point to the need for counselors to advocate for the needs of older adults and their families, we want to caution against treating older adults merely as people to be served. Advocacy may mean helping older adults advocate for themselves as well as intervening for them. By definition, older adults are survivors, and one of our jobs as counselors and advocates is to help them identify and utilize the repertoire of coping skills they have developed over a lifetime.

Advocacy strategies

To advocate for older adults, we first need first to be knowledgeable about the needs and concerns of this population and familiar with the aging network which encompasses the array of services for older adults. For example, we should know how to contact the Eldercare Locator, a national organization that describes itself as "A way to find community assistance for seniors." (Contact information for all of the groups mentioned are at the end of the article.) It is also important to have contacts with the Area Agency on Aging or local service providers who can effectively direct older adults or family members through the maze of services.

We have divided advocacy strategies into four areas. First, we need to teach clients advocacy skills and attitudes so that they can advocate for themselves. Second, we need to work with existing organizations at the national, state, and local levels. Third, we need to advocate at the political level, with local, state, and national legislatures and other governmental bodies. And fourth, we often need to advocate for recognition of the special needs of the elderly with institutions that serve the general population.

Help older adults to advocate for themselves
It is important that we not belittle older adults by assuming that we must "take care of" them. An important role for us may be to help older adults learn advocacy strategies, including appropriately assertive behaviors. Age cohort issues may arise here as many of today's older adults are part of a tradition of independence. Often this includes a "don't make waves" approach.

Previous generations often saw needing assistance beyond the family as a sign of weakness or vulnerability. Different cultures have different terms for this idea of protecting privacy. "Don't air your dirty linen in public" is a common one. Among Jewish families the statement "It's a shonda for the goyim" expressed the idea that it would bring shame if a Jew ever let "outsiders" know about their unmet needs. Other families express their pride in independence with such statements as "I kept food on the table during the Depression; my family was never hungry."

Helping older adults with these kinds of traditions understand their entitlements can be an important role for helpers/advocates. As today's younger people age, these kinds of issues may disappear. But we suspect that the strong independence value fostered in American culture will continue to influence many people and make it harder for them when some sort of dependence becomes necessary. Abused elders may need special assistance as they may not be aware of their rights and/or may be afraid to ask for help because they perceive themselves as dependent on their abusers.

Assisting older adults advocate for themselves can take many forms. Coaching or role playing may help individuals (caregivers as well as older adults themselves) ask for what they need from health care providers, public and private bureaucracies or other organizations. Assertiveness training may help groups of older adults develop needed skills. For example, the center at which we both worked offered a class called "Growing Older Bolder." Groups of older adults can also be taught, or reminded to use, political advocacy and community organizing skills. Remember that many trade unions, and important advocacy groups were started by people who are today "older adults."

Work with existing organizations
Here are several suggestions for contacting and working with other organizations.

- Counselor advocates should contact the aging network in their community or state for information on available services. Federal funding for services for older adults is funneled through state offices of aging and regional area agencies on aging, known as AAA's. In planning distribution of these funds, AAA's hold annual hearings which represent an excellent opportunity to advocate for those services your clients most need. Such contacts also present an opportunity to advocate for licensing for facilities that serve older adults, and for standards of staff training and performance.
- One important entry point for counselor advocates is to locate coalitions of mental health and aging organizations at the national, state, and local level. The National Coalition on Mental Health and Aging includes representatives of:
  1) Professional associations, such as ACA, NASW, APA, ASA (The American Society on Aging) and NCOA (the National Council on Aging);
  2) Government organizations, such as the Administration on Aging, the National Association of State Units on Aging, the National Association of Area Agencies on Aging, and the National Institute of Mental Health;
  3) Aging organizations, such as AARP, the National

Council of Senior Citizens, and the National Caucus and Center on Black Aged.

Many states have similar coalitions that can be contacted through the state department of aging and/or mental health department. At the local level it may be easiest to contact the Area Agency on Aging.

- Locate, recommend, and publicize innovative services. Two examples follow:

  1) In some communities the Eden Alternative represents an approach to long term care designed to make facilities more like homes and less like institutions. Nursing homes that adapt this approach bring pets and plants into the facility, and give residents responsibility for their care. Young children are typically brought in to engage in joint activities with residents.

  2) Other communities are experimenting with providing mental health services in physical health care settings. Such an approach is designed to address the reluctance of many older adults to seek traditional mental health services. To evaluate this approach, the U.S. Substance Abuse and Mental Health Services has provided a number of grants to assess the effectiveness of this kind of integrated model of treatment in the primary care setting itself.

- In addition to working through professional contacts we recommend that advocates work with organizations which represent older adults. For example:

  1) AARP is one of the largest membership organizations in this country, with an active corps of volunteers, newsletters, and magazines which reflect the interests of members, and a staff which lobbies on behalf of those members. Both the Washington office and regional offices will supply information and contacts.

  2) A much smaller organization, the Older Women's League (OWL), has a platform which calls for: a national universal health care system, economic security including social security and pensions, full access to appropriate housing and housing alternatives, ending violence against women and the elderly, staying in control through all of life,

and combating discrimination in the work place. OWL has a Washington office and local chapters throughout the country. Its current president, Betty Lee Ongley from Michigan, is a good example of a retired counselor serving as an advocate.

Advocate at the Political Level

Political advocacy takes many forms. As individuals, we can monitor proposed legislation at the national and state level which would affect benefits and services for older adults and let our views be known. For example, the news media is currently full of ideas for revamping social security programs, often with a view toward privatization. Counselors need to be aware that such proposals may negate the safety net provided by Social Security, particularly for women. Twice as many women as men rely on Social Security for at least 90% of their income. Women of color are even more likely to live in poverty than are white women.

Another much discussed issue of extreme importance to older adults concerns financing of health care. When HMOs decide they cannot afford to serve older adults, a crisis is at hand which necessitates broad based advocacy. Medicare and Medicaid only partially fill this gap.

To maximize our impact it is important to work with some of the groups that already do political advocacy. We have already mentioned one very large group, AARP, and one small group, OWL. Both have lobbyists in Washington and chapters in local areas. Our own ACA, and in particular one of its divisions, (AADA) the Association for Adult Development and Aging, address issues of older adults when they intersect with the with the needs of counselors or the services counselors can provide. Working with such organizations is crucial to successful political advocacy. It is one way to work to include age in all non-discriminatory statements.

Miscellaneous Client Advocacy

As we consider how life can be improved for many older adults, it is important to think broadly about the many entities with which they interact. Service locations from grocery stores to department stores, libraries to senior centers, and social security offices to doctor's offices, need to be aware of, and responsive to, normal age related sensory losses. Such responsiveness should involve making sure that printed material is easy to read, that auditory distractions are minimized, and that chairs are firm and easy to get in and out of.

An important role for counselors/advocates might be to encourage managers at all kinds of facilities to ask their older consumers what would make their services more hospitable. We might hear about needs for better lighting, wider aisles to accommodate wheel chairs, or programs held during daylight hours and accessible by good public transportation. Many older adults enjoy attending classes and artistic performances. Some may need reduced tuition or admission fees.

Possibly a major way we can be better advocates is to picture ourselves as older adults and consider what would make our lives less complicated and more fulfilling. What could we do for ourselves with the assistance of groups of various kinds? The challenge for us then is to determine how can we make that happen for the adults whom we serve. It is our hope that the information in this piece will make it easier for you to enter into advocacy roles.

Suggested Resources:

Professional Associations:
ASA (The American Society on Aging)
833 Market Street, Suite 511, San Francisco, CA 94103.
Phone: (415) 974-9600
Web site: asaging.org
(This organization includes a Mental Health and Aging
  Network)

NCOA (National Council on Aging)
409 Third Street, SW
Washington, DC 20024
Phone: (202) 479-1200

Membership and Advocacy Organizations:
AARP (The American Association of Retired Persons)
601 E Street, NW Washington, D.C. 20049
Phone: (202) 434-2277
Web site: www.aarp.org

Bazelon Center for Mental Health Law
(This group is helping older consumers of mental health

services form a new advocacy organization.)
1101 15th St, NW-Suite 1212
Washington, DC 20005
(202) 467-5730
www:bazelon.org

Gray Panthers
3635 Chestnut Street
Philadelphia, PA 19104

National Caucus and Center on Black Aged
1424 K Street, NW
Washington, DC
(202) 637-8400

OWL (Older Women's League)
666 11th Street, NW, Suite 700
Washington, DC 20001
(202) 783-6686 or 1-800-0825-3695

Recommended Reading

The AARP Guide to Internet Resources Related to Aging.
Available from AARP (mailing address above) or through
www.aarp.org/cyber/guide1.htm

A comprehensive listing of websites divided into such categories
as world wide web, government and government related, health
related, housing and living arrangements, income-related, law-
related, leisure activities, and social services. Also includes
listings for listservs, usenet newsgroups, newsletters, and
electronic magazines related to aging.

Wacker, R.R., Roberto, K.A., & Piper, L.E. (1998) *Community
Resources for Older Adults: Programs and Services in an Era of
Change.* Thousand Oaks, CA: Pine Forge Press

A useful overview of the legislative basis for programs, services,
and benefits for older adults. Chapters on various services (e.g.
information and referral, senior centers and recreation, respite
services, and nursing homes) contain descriptions of services,
examples of best practices, case studies, national organizations,

and Internet resources for each topic area.

Jane Goodman is an associate professor at Oakland University in Rochester, Mich. Elinor Waters is a training consultant in Chevy Chase, Md.

Chapter Nine

Social Justice Advocacy with Lesbian, Bisexual, Gay, and Transgendered Persons

Stuart F. Chen-Hayes

"I've been harassed in my school. It's been physical sometimes. It's been bad. I've reported it and nothing's been done. This year when I go back to school, if I get harassed and nothing happens I'm on my school's case from now on. I've learned I have rights and I don't have to put up with that. I'm just now saying "Hey, forget this!"
Renee, a lesbian youth, quoted in *Free Your Mind* (1996)

"I attended the memorial march in honor of Matthew Shepard's horrible death to protest hate crimes. As I watched some NYPD officers kick, beat, and use horses to attack the peaceful marchers, I was beyond rage. In reflecting on the police officers' production of violence during a civilian anti-violence march, I realized the United States structurally uses fear and force through public and private institutions to keep us queers down, out, and anything but equal."
A gay man of transgender experience at the October 1998 Matthew Shepard political funeral in New York City

LGBT Advocacy 101

Lesbian, bisexual, gay, and transgendered (LBGT) clients, co-workers, and community members are often daily targets of oppression in schools, organizations, and communities. They are subjected to this oppression based on their nondominant sexual orientations, gender identities or both (Bass & Kaufman, 1996; Blumenfeld, 1992; Broun & Rounsley, 1996; Pharr, 1988, 1996; Barret, 1998). Professional counselors of diverse sexual orientations and gender identities are an excellent advocacy resource for LBGT persons challenging oppression.

The American Counseling Association's Code of Ethics and Standards of Practice (ACA, 1995) encourages counselors to affirm clients' sexual orientation. *Sexual orientation* can be defined as a multivariable dynamic that includes past, present, and ideal feelings about who is attractive, or desirable in sexual and romantic ways or both. It can include one's sexual attractions, behaviors, fantasies, gender emotional preference, gender social preference, sexual identity in a community (lesbian, bisexual, gay, or heterosexual), and use of a sexual identity self-label (Klein, Sepekoff, & Wolf, 1985). There is no definitive answer for how sexual orientation occurs; it is on a continuum and can be fluid or fixed over a person's lifetime. The term *sexual preference*, in contrast, is vague and unhelpful as it implies that persons choose their orientation and many people believe they did not choose their sexual orientation (Dworkin & Gutierrez, 1992; Barret, 1998).

Although sexual orientation is addressed in the ACA Code of Ethics and Standards of Practice, gender identity is not. *Gender identity* is a person's internal, subjective experience of how he or she feels as a "gendered" person in terms of gender roles, attitudes, and behaviors. It may or may not "match" a person's genitals, clothing, or other gendered signals and cues. A person's gender identity is based on various personal, social, and cultural factors.

Heterosexism and *transgenderism* are the forms of oppression that relate to violence against and hatred of people in the nondominant group in terms of both sexual orientation (lesbians, bisexuals, and gay men) or gender identity (transgendered persons including transsexuals, cross-dressers, intersexuals, drag queens, drag kings, and so forth). Heterosexism is the use of prejudice multiplied by power used by members of the dominant sexual orientation (heterosexual) toward members of nondominant sexual orientations (lesbian, bisexual, and gay) to restrict their access to resources (individual, cultural, and institutional/systemic). Transgenderism is prejudice multiplied by power used by traditionally gendered persons toward nontraditionally gendered persons (transgendered, transsexual, cross-dressers, intersexuals, drag queens, and drag kings) to restrict their access to resources (individual, cultural, and institutional/systemic).

Acknowledging and Challenging Heterosexual and Traditionally Gendered Privileges

There are many ways for a professional counselor to be an advocate with lesbian, bisexual, gay, and transgendered persons. One way for heterosexual and traditionally gendered persons to challenge heterosexism and transgenderism is to develop awareness and knowledge about the privileges that they enjoy as heterosexual and traditionally gendered people in our society. The following list identifies just a small portion of the privileges enjoyed by heterosexuals and traditionally gendered persons:

- No mental health or medical "professionals" advocate against heterosexual or traditionally gendered persons as mentally ill or in need of conversion therapies or reversal of "gender dysphoria"
- Ability to be affectionate in public without fear of retribution, harassment, or other forms of violence for heterosexuals and traditionally gendered persons
- Legal recognition of life commitments/partnerships for heterosexuals
- Health care/bereavement benefits with legally sanctioned marriage for heterosexuals
- No worry about loss of a job, friendship or family due to one's sexual orientation or gender identity
- Hospital visiting privileges for heterosexuals
- Ability to become a citizen through marriage for heterosexuals
- Ability to see positive images of heterosexual and traditionally gendered persons in all walks of life from earliest age until older years throughout the culture, media, and institutions, etc.
- No organized, well-financed religious and political opposition to heterosexuality and traditionally gendered persons
- One's children would not be taken away or visitation privileges restricted or denied due to being heterosexual or traditionally gendered
- No fear of being "outed" as heterosexual or traditionally gendered in workplaces, communities, cultures, or families where being open with one's sexual orientation is dangerous
- No need to educate others about what it means to be heterosexual or traditionally gendered

- Ability to gain and share credit as heterosexual or traditionally gendered married couples
- No discrimination in housing, securing loans, or in seeking public accommodations due to being heterosexual or traditionally gendered
- No fear of losing one's job due to being heterosexual or traditionally gendered
- Tax and inheritance/survivorship benefits for married same-gendered couples
- Service providers and strangers automatically assume that members of a couple or singles are traditionally gendered or heterosexual.
- When discussing dating or sexual experiences, heterosexuals and traditionally gendered persons are never accused of "flaunting it."

Once people have become aware of their privilege, they can begin to develop skills that challenge them, especially as they oppress LBGT persons.

It is important for professional counselors interested in LBGT advocacy to have direct experiences with LBGT persons in a variety of professional and personal situations. Direct personal contact involving LBGT persons as the "experts" on heterosexism and transgenderism is a powerful device for listening and learning. It provides a chance for heterosexual and traditionally gendered advocates to hone their awareness, knowledge, and skills so that LBGT persons don't have to always assume the lead in challenging heterosexism and transgenderism.

Specific LBGT Advocacy Issues

Gay, bisexual, and transgendered men are disproportionately targeted by police for entrapment due to their sexual orientation. Lesbian, bisexual, and transgendered women are prone to invisibility in a culture that erases their existence in many contexts, such as the lack of health care research conducted on lesbian, bisexual, and transgendered women. Bisexual persons are targeted with shame/stigma by persons who don't believe bisexuals exist or that they are untrustworthy or lying about their sexual orientation. Transgendered persons are subject to loss of jobs, lack of health care coverage, and constant pressure to subscribe to a binary pattern of gender identity, appearance, and expression. Many LBGT persons in families are subject to harassment, abandonment, and abuse. LBGT persons in same-gender relationships lack civil rights and protections that heterosexual persons receive through legal marriage.

Because of the additive nature of multiple oppressions (Dworkin & Gutierrez, 1992; Pharr, 1988), people with additional nondominant cultural identities may be the targets of multiple forms of persecution. Among the LBGT persons who may be subjected to intense forms of oppression are persons of color, persons with disabilities, youth and older persons, poor and working class persons; persons with nondominant religious/ spiritual identities, women and girls, persons who speak English as a second language, with an accent, or not at all, noncitizens, single parents and other nontraditional family types, and persons with nondominant appearances. Culturally competent advocates in counseling take all of a person's cultural identities into account when collaborating on advocacy strategies.

Advocacy Against Internalized and Externalized Oppression

One of the most powerful ways that oppression operates for members of nondominant groups is that when people hear myths and stereotypes about themselves long enough, or when they don't have access to accurate information, or when they are subjected to repeated acts of trauma and violence they begin to believe the lies, myths, and stereotypes about themselves and members of their group, in this case, LBGT persons. They take responsibility for the myths and stereotypes and internalize them, or begin to believe them, which is what is known as internalized oppression (Chen-Hayes, 1997; Arnold & Lewis, 1998).

This may lead to LBGT persons: violating each other, isolation, increased chemical dependency, invisibility, guilt, shame, sex and gender negativity, dishonesty, believing that violence is the price one has to pay to be LBGT, and other forms of self-hatred. Externalized oppression is what is done, consciously or unconsciously, by members of dominant sexual orientations and gender identities to keep resources out of the hands of LBGT persons. It can be done on individual, cultural, and systemic/ institutional levels. Advocates for LBGT persons have many actions they can take to challenge externalized oppression.

Advocacy strategies for counselors on the individual level include:
- writing a letter or visiting an elected representative to promote hate crimes legislation, and other forms of civil

rights protections for LBGT persons, couples, and families; challenging myths and stereotypes about lesbian, bisexual, gay, and transgendered persons (Chen-Hayes, 1997; Barret, 1998);

- interrupting hateful "jokes" about LBGT persons; giving accurate information about LBGT persons (Lewis & Arnold, 1998);
- having books and images in one's office/workplace that give a clear, affirming message about LBGT persons; ensuring that written and intake forms and spoken language used by school and agency personnel use inclusive language like partner instead of husband/wife or spouse and never assume a child, adolescent or adult's sexual orientation or gender identity; becoming an ally by taking on the struggles of LBGT persons (Lewis & Arnold, 1998).

On the cultural level, advocacy strategies include:
- inviting LBGT persons to be guest speakers in schools and agencies;
- using LBGT persons throughout the curriculum in all parts of the educational system (K-12 and in universities);
- subscribing to cable TV, magazines, newspapers, radio stations, and other forms of media that showcase LBGT persons without bias or stereotypes;
- supporting arts and cultural workers who showcase LBGT persons and cultural work;
- ensuring local community and school libraries have books and magazines that feature LBGT books and LBGT authors for all ages with content that is developmentally appropriate (SIECUS, 1996).

Advocacy strategies on the systemic level include:
- promoting a sex education curriculum in schools that is comprehensive, collaboratively designed with parents, teacher and administrators, and LBGT-affirming (SIECUS, 1996);
- creating a gay/straight (and bi/lesbian transgender) alliance in your school, agency, or community; creating a workplace or school or agency statement that creates a hate-free zone with zero tolerance for any/all oppressions/violence;
- developing work-related LBGT and ally support groups; developing a local chapter of PFLAG (Parents and

Friends of Lesbians and Gays) or GLSEN (Gay, Lesbian, Straight Education Network), both of whom are bisexual and transgender inclusive;
- creating and promoting legislation to reduce hate crimes and promote civil rights protection for persons of all sexual orientations and gender identities;
- challenging the medicalization of nondominant sexual orientations and nontraditional gender identities as pathological or sick;
- challenging religious organizations that oppress LBGT persons as "sinful" or "evil."

Conclusion

Professional counselors can play major leadership roles in advocacy by addressing issues at the individual, cultural, and institutional/systemic levels. They can work closely with their client-colleagues to challenge both internalized and externalized forms of oppression. The resources that counselors can use in this effort are many and varied, as the following list of World Wide Web resources demonstrates.

LBGT Advocacy Web Resources

AGLBIC—Association for Gay, Lesbian, and Bisexual Issues in Counseling aglbic.org

BINET—Bisexual Network of the United States— www.binetusa.org

Bisexual Resource Center— www.biresource.org

IFGE—International Foundation for Gender Education www.ifge.org

Intersex Voices—www.qis.net/~triea/

PFLAG—Parents, Families, and Friends of Lesbians and Gays www.pflag.org

GLSEN—Gay, Lesbian, and Straight Education Network www.glsen.org

Lambda Legal Defense and Education Fund— www.lambdalegal.org

National Black Gay and Lesbian Leadership Forum — www.nblglf.org

National Center for Lesbian Rights— www.nclrights.org

National Latina/o Lesbian, Gay, Bisexual, and Transgender Organization —www.llego.org

!OUTPROUD! National Coalition for Gay, Lesbian, Bisexual, and Transgender Youth— www.outproud.org

SIECUS—Sex Education and Information Council of the United States—www.siecus.org

References

American Counseling Association (1995). Code of Ethics and Standards of Practice. Alexandria, VA: American Counseling Association.

Barret, B. (1998). Gay and lesbian activism: A frontier in social advocacy. In C. C. Lee & G. R. Walz, (Eds.), Social action: A mandate for counselors (pp. 83-98). Alexandria, VA: American Counseling Association and ERIC Counseling and Student Services Clearinghouse.

Bass, E., & Kaufman, K. (1996). Free your mind: The book for gay, lesbian, and bisexual youth—and their allies. New York, NY: HarperCollins.

Blumenfeld, W. (Ed.). (1992). Homophobia: How we all pay the price. Boston, MA: Beacon Press.

Brown, M. I., & Rounsley, C. A. (1996). Understanding transsexualism: For families, friends, coworkers, and helping professionals. San Francisco: Jossey-Bass.

Chen-Hayes, S. F. (1997). Counseling lesbian, bisexual, and gay persons in couple and family relationships: Overcoming the stereotypes. The Family Journal: Counseling and Therapy for Couples and Families 5(3), 236-240.

Dworkin, S. & Gutierrez, F. (1992). Counseling gay men and lesbians: Journey to the end of the rainbow. Alexandria, VA: American Counseling Association

Klein, F., Sepekoff, B., & Wolf, T. J. (1985). "Sexual orientation: A multi-variable dynamic process." In F. Klein & T. J. Wolf, (Eds.). Two lives to lead: Bisexuality in men and women. New York: Harrington Park Press.

Lewis, J. A., & Arnold, M. S. (1998). From multiculturalism to social action. In C. C. Lee & G. R. Walz, (Eds.), Social action: A mandate for counselors (pp. 51-66). Alexandria, VA: American Counseling Association and ERIC Counseling and Student Services Clearinghouse.

National Guidelines Task Force.(1996). Guidelines for comprehensive sexuality education (2nd Ed.). New York: Sex Information and Education Council of the United States.

Pharr, S. (1996). In the time of the right: Reflections on liberation. Little Rock, AR: Chardon Press.

Pharr, S. (1988). Homophobia: A weapon of sexism. Little Rock, AR: Chardon Press.

Stuart F. Chen-Hayes, Ph.D., N.C.C., is an Assistant Professor in the Department of Specialized Services, Graduate Program in Counseling, at Lehman College of the City University of New York.

Chapter Ten

Gender-based Advocacy for Equity and Non-violence

Sunny Hansen

Should counselors today be concerned about gender roles and gender-based issues? Haven't we solved all the gender-based problems with the extensive interventions of the last 25 years? My answers to these questions are a resounding yes to the first and no to the second. I will discuss gender advocacy, and the values assumptions undergirding it, largely in relation to equity and non-violence. Advocacy strategies and resources appear throughout the paper.

The Need for Gender-Based Advocacy

While the U.S. has made considerable progress in reducing sexism, gender bias, and gender discrimination, there is still a long way to go to create a society of gender equity and non-violence which will reduce oppressions, expand options, and remove barriers to opportunity for girls and boys of all backgrounds. Although there are those who do not want to believe there is still a problem, indications from many studies, publications, and men's and women's "lived experience" are that gender barriers and issues still exist. They have been minimized perhaps because, while we have become aware of multiple forms of discrimination, gender discrimination seems less important. Although all forms of violence are deplorable, violence against women persists in spite of changing laws and norms which try to reduce it, e.g. sexual harassment, rape and sexual assault, and domestic battering.

Unique issues exist with regard to gender and multicultural counseling. In spite of controversy over whether multiculturalism should be defined narrowly or broadly, the multicultural literature is increasingly inclusive, defining the multiple dimensions of identity as race, ethnicity, class, gender, religion, sexual orientation, age, disability, and language. Gender identity is one of the dimensions still important to many men and women, but it must be examined in relation to the salience of other forms of identity to a particular person. It is unfortunate, I believe, that although gender is a thread which runs through all cultures, it often is not recognized as an issue. Postmodern thinkers suggest that gender is a characteristic which has been constructed by society, that it has caused us to inappropriately focus on gender differences, and that it should be deconstructed. This school of thought is similar in some ways to those who suggest that individuals gain gender knowledge early in life, develop dichotomous thinking about male and female roles, and need to transcend them so that all individuals will have access to the full range of emotions, feelings, and behaviors—and I would add, opportunities.

Advocacy is needed to combat violence against women and devaluing of women, as well as in salary and promotion differentials, occupational segregation, and in gender-biased counseling. While gender issues have been perceived as "women's issues" for many decades, there is beginning recognition of issues unique to boys and men. The most frequently mentioned male problems are with reading and writing, aggressive behavior, dropping out of school, incarceration, and restricted emotionality. An assumption of this article is that gender role issues affect both sexes and that both boys and girls need to be free of violence and discrimination, have opportunities to consider all options, develop their potentials, contribute to community, and become self-sufficient, connected, and respected human beings.

Barriers Based on Gender

An abundance of contextual data shows that negative stereotypes and socialization continue to create barriers for girls of all backgrounds, in spite of progress in inclusion and representation of formerly excluded and underrepresented groups. These barriers are exacerbated for women and girls of color or disability. Yet a proliferation of sports bars, adult shows, "sex entertainment" bars, certain TV programs, and web pornography, along with predominantly male faces in Congress, government, corporations, and board rooms, remind us of the dominant male values in positions of power and of sexist attitudes which still prevail and keep women from taking their place as equal partners.

Although more than half of U.S. women are in the workforce

in every state except West Virginia, and they have greater access to such fields as medicine, law, finance, veterinary medicine, accounting, and dentistry, they continue to dominate in traditional women's fields of study (e.g., education, childcare, nursing, and office work). They are still underrepresented in the hard science fields such as physics, engineering and computer technology; salaries are not equitable for women and men working in the same field, and white collar women earn 72% compared to their male counterparts. On the other hand, men are also victims of violence; they are not rushing into nurturing, caring fields, partly because caring is not valued, the pay is less, and stereotypes continue about what is appropriate as women's work and men's work. Work and family conflicts in two-earner heterosexual families continue to be viewed as women's issues.

Mixed Signs of Progress

That progress in gender issues such as educational equity has been made for women is illustrated most dramatically by the fact that women now surpass men in percentages in college graduate and undergraduate programs. By 2008, if the trend continues, college women will outnumber men by 9.2 million to 6.9 million. One reason for this is that men are choosing to enter the high-paying computer jobs for which they are being sought and skipping a college education. What this portends for the future is uncertain in terms of relationships between women and men and men's preparation for roles in family, parenting, and citizenship. Instrumental values of computer technology are being stressed in such recruiting, and expressive values of women again seem to be considered less important. One author recently suggested that having more women on campus should not be a concern. He asks, "Is the overrepresentation of women in agriculture a bigger problem than their underrepresentation in technology? He suggests that if women reach parity with men in higher education, "they are also likely to make greater strides in the professions, and we will have to learn to live with a world of increasing gender equality."

I would in no way suggest that gender is always the primary equity issue. Valerie Lee and her associates at the University of Michigan analyzed the National Educational Longitudinal Study (NELS) data on eighth and tenth graders and concluded that, although gender equity is still a problem, social class was a greater barrier to opportunity than either race or gender.

While there is evidence that both sexes are affected by gender equity issues, recent documents still focus mainly on the educational status and opportunity of girls and women. In the 1990s a number of publications of the American Association of University Women documented several aspects of gender equity for women. The most controversial was *How Schools Shortchange Girls* (1992), which conducted a thorough review of literature and studied both girls and boys, including children of color. *Hostile Hallways* (1995) studied sexual harassment and found a majority of both boys and girls experienced harassment at some time in their schools. What schools are doing to help girls succeed is reported in *GROWING SMART: What's Working for Girls in Schools* (1995) in which the authors suggest that themes important to girls (e.g. identity, centrality, caring adults, academic achievement, and opportunity to realize dreams) often are also important to boys. The authors also emphasize that systems interventions involving students, parents, school personnel, and community are essential.

The most recent study, *Gender Gaps: Where Schools Still Fail Our Children* (1998), provides strong evidence of both progress and a continuing need for school-based and community-based interventions. Researchers state that equitable education usually implies quality education and equal opportunities for all students and addresses the needs of both girls and boys. They found that class organization, teaching styles, teacher-student interactions, role models, and equipment tend to favor boys. They also found persistent problems in areas such as course-taking patterns, assessment, standards, extracurricular activities, and career choice. A study on the *Educational Status of Girls and Women in the Nation* was due to be presented to Congress on January 1, 1999, but it was not yet available from the Equity Resource Center at Newton, Massachusetts, at this writing. What is needed now are more studies of the role and status of both boys and girls, their interactive effects, and creative interventions for both.

Rationale for Advocacy

Evidence of the need for advocacy of gender equity for our clients is embedded in much of what has been said above. All the problems of achieving gender equity and reducing violence and multiple forms of discrimination have not been solved in spite of the hundreds of interventions developed and implemented since the 70s. Issues of inequity, female subordination, socialization, and stereotyping are so ingrained that they do not disappear in one generation. Efforts to get women (and men) into nontraditional occupations have not been entirely successful.

Gender in Historical Context

It is about 25 years since the Women's Educational Equity Act (WEEA) and Title IX were passed to provide girls and women educational equity and prohibit discrimination in educational institutions. Although great progress has been made in areas such as sports, even there inequities and stereotypes continue, as the University of Minnesota Tucker Center on Girls and Women in Sports attests. Other legislation such as Equal Employment Opportunity, Sexual Harassment, and Affirmative Action Executive Orders (now under fire in some states) was enacted to ensure the rights of specific groups. Because women comprise more than half of these populations, gender issues are involved in all of them. Non-governmental organizations also have been created to address specific issues, such as women's centers, rape and sexual assault centers, battered women's centers, and a few men's centers. While the U.S. is farther along than some countries on a continuum of change, there is still much to do to eliminate the now more subtle forms of gender bias.

A Systems Intervention Strategy

Because gender equity was viewed as a "women's issue" in the 1970s, little attention was paid to boys. One intervention for both girls and boys which has continued is the BORN FREE Program at the University of Minnesota, a national counseling-based program built around the concepts of career development, gender role stereotyping and socialization, and educational and social change. Its assumptions are that negative stereotyping affects both sexes, that no one is to blame because it is part of our socialization, that stereotypes and other barriers exist at home, in the media, in our communities, and throughout the educational spectrum, and that since both men and women are affected, both need to work on the problems.

BORN FREE's purpose is to Build Options, Reassess Norms, and Free Roles through Educational Equity. It is an indirect intervention, creating videos and print materials to train educators and parents on how to reduce career-related sex-role stereotyping, expand options for both girls and boys, and teach participants how to be change agents in their own institutions. It is an advocacy program. One of the first programs funded under WEEA, it involved

14 educational institutions K-college and faculty and graduate students in counseling, higher education, and teacher education. They developed and piloted the materials to reduce the barriers and increase the facilitators of career development of both sexes. The BORN FREE videos, training packets, literature reviews, and change process reports were disseminated by WEEA for 14 years, an unusually long shelf life. Funds are now being sought to update them. Although on a skeletal budget, BORN FREE recently has been re-envisioned as a center for applied research and interventions and expanded to focus on gender, culture, and career. It also has an international electronic listserv with subscribers from many countries.

Many new teachers (including counselors) being trained today have not had the exposure to gender equity training common in the 70s. Gender equity is simply not as visible or important a topic in elementary, secondary, or higher education. Direct interventions with students themselves are needed at all levels, and indirect interventions such as many developed in the 70s are also needed. Girls and boys need to learn early in life to work as partners in reducing problems of violence, inequity and other social justice issues in their own institutions and communities.

Gender Advocacy Across Cultures

There are many reasons that gender advocacy is needed across cultures. Societies are changing, demographics are changing, workplaces are changing, families are changing, and gender roles are changing. Increasingly we are realizing that we need to change systems to meet individual needs and not change individuals to fit society or the status quo. Challenging issues exist when the norms and values of immigrants from other cultures clash with majority of Western cultures, especially in relation to gender roles and family norms. Gender issues exist across global cultures, and it is essential that counselors and counselor educators develop a global perspective about them. In some cultures the problems are more severe and extreme. For example, few counselors, if they have any commitment to human rights and democratic freedoms, would condone the violence against women by the Taliban in Afghanistan. Some call it "gendercide." Violence against women has been institutionalized to the extent that women are being raped, put in prison, and totally dehumanized. They cannot go to school, practice medicine, use male doctors to get medical care for themselves or their children, or expose any part of their body. Issues of infanticide, dowry bride burning, (and hate crimes in the U.S.) and inequality in education, law, health, and property are other global examples. These are clearly human rights issues.

In spite of our need to respect culture, it is important to help our students and professionals understand that there some universal or superordinate values which transcend culture, values that have to do with democratic principles of human dignity and respect. With the growing ACA interest in international issues and collaboration, some form of outreach to Afghan women, and other dehumanized women, is imperative. One political strategy is to lobby Congress to ratify the United Nations Convention to Eliminate All forms of Discrimination against Women.

Intervention for Boys and Men

While gender roles affect men as well as women, there have not been as many interventions to help men change their role or status. Joseph Pleck, James O'Neil, Thomas Skovholt, and Murray Sher are among the few counseling psychologists who have addressed male issues such as male gender role strain, men's role in the family, men's career and economic issues, aggression, and emotionality issues. Perhaps the most publicized interventions are those to assist Black males, such as those developed by Courtland Lee (1989). Besides the religious-based Promise Keepers, who advocate women's subordinate status and the dominance of men, special initiatives have been created to help men become more nurturing, express feelings, resolve conflicts, become better fathers, and become involved in child care, especially as custodial fathers.

Gender-Based Advocacy Strategies

Counselors can be advocates for diverse clients affected by gender oppression as they can for other kinds of problems. The young high school girl being harassed by boys (or other girls) needs someone to support her. The adolescent girl who is anorexic or bulimic needs help from sensitive well-trained counselors and other mental health professionals skilled in addressing these psychological and body image issues. The victim of rape needs to know that caring persons in the legal and social services system understand the trauma she has experienced and can help her develop a counseling plan for recovery. The battered woman needs a support group and agencies, counselors, and social workers who can help her survive emotionally, move beyond the victim status, get legal assistance, housing, child care and a job—and escape the situation if it cannot be changed. Resilience in battered women has been documented, but the women need to know the system is working for, not against them. Clients of both sexes experience trauma and stress and need help from gender-aware, culturally sensitive counselors.

Continuing Advocacy for Girls and Women

The most important strategies are those which are preventive. As the above narrative illustrates, a great deal has been done in the last quarter century, but what is there left to do?

- Across cultures, while women have made progress in education and health, they remain underrepresented in government and business, especially at top levels. Political activism is needed to gain more diversity in top policy-making bodies and boards.
- Women still have a long way to go to achieve equity in the hard sciences, engineering, and computer technology. Programs to increase computer literacy and competencies of girls and women need to grow. Those such as the Computer Equity Expert Project Jo Sanders developed in Manhattan (1993) provide an excellent model.
- Women are still greatly underrepresented in the trades, where many of the highly paid jobs are. Helping girls and women choose and prepare for "nontraditional jobs" is still a big challenge. Unfortunately, many initiatives funded under the School to Work Act are not helping gender equity, in spite of equity requirements in the 1994 Act. It is quite ironic that, while the U.S. Congress has appropriated millions of dollars for STW, the WEEA allocation for 1999 was $600,000. As school counselors work more closely with curriculum and systematic interventions, they can become agents of change in programs that promote equity and non-violence, as well as gender-fair career development, for girls and boys of all backgrounds.
- In sports participation as well as observation, the U.S. is still a male-dominated culture (witness the Super Bowl mania). Politically working toward more balance in sports participation and appropriations is one strategy.

Encouraging girls and women to develop physical skills and team participation is another. Providing role models, striving to eliminate stereotypes of women in sports, and challenging TV and other media portrayals are others.

- Overall we still have a sex-segregated society, in the workplace and in some parts of education, and in leisure activities. Problems increase for older adults, especially women, as myths and stereotypes still prevail. Counseling interventions are needed to reduce violence, create opportunities, and increase accuracy in portrayal, balance, and representation of girls and women of all backgrounds.

New Advocacy for Boys and Men

Some of the earlier statements about systems interventions and advocacy apply to boys as well as to girls, though the differential power in relationships, work, and educational systems needs to be kept in mind. Possible strategies for reducing negative stereotypes affecting male socialization include the following:

- Develop school and college programs designed to help boys and young men deal with their unique needs and issues, e.g. how to succeed in nontraditional roles, how to communicate better, how to show affection, how to control aggression, how to deal with changes in women's roles. One example is to integrate age-appropriate guidance units on boys' developmental issues at different educational levels.
- Advocate for the importance of getting a college education and a liberal education in order to become whole persons before succumbing to recruiters for computer jobs.
- Develop mentor programs so boys and young men are exposed to a variety of lifestyles, including men in egalitarian roles.
- Create learning experiences in which boys can work in nontraditional roles such as child care assistant or volunteer in a nursing home.
- Teach boys conflict resolution and mediation to avoid violence, especially against women; also to show empathy and stand up for victims of trauma, especially rape, sexual assault, and battering.
- Incorporate knowledge of such topics as stereotyping and socialization, domestic violence, and equity into teacher and counselor education programs.

- Advocate for legislation for a MEEP—Men's Educational Equity Program— to educate boys and men—but not taking still needed funds away from women.
- Develop preventive programs for boys at risk and likely to drop out, have learning or emotional difficulties, or end up homeless or in the correctional system.
- Teach boys that the very real gender role changes in society may mean positive gains for men as well as women. This will become more evident as women and men tell their stories—especially of their relationships as equal partners.

Advocacy Strategies for Both Sexes

Although gender issues were virtually left out of educational reform of the 1980s, it is important that they not be left out again in the 90s. Unfortunately the linear and instrumental focus of school-to-work programs which dominate educational reform at present threatens again. Below are a few additional strategies which counselors can use for both sexes.

- Help girls and boys, men and women understand their rights under the law—whether sexual harassment, pay equity, bias and discrimination in education, counseling, or work.
- Help both boys and girls get involved in action learning and service learning in which they can share roles and function as equals to remove some of the stereotypes and contribute to community.
- Help both understand that old stereotyped roles—girls as nurturers and boys as providers—limit the development of both and that both need self-sufficiency and connectedness.
- Help both to work on eliminating oppressions related to being male and female.
- Collaborate with teachers to create units for both sexes on work and family.
- Teach both girls and boys nonviolent conflict resolution and mediation.
- Advocate for systems change (schools, colleges, and workplaces) which foster student development for broad life roles and options.
- Provide models of equality and egalitarian relationships that help girls and boys of all backgrounds to treat each

other as equals and with respect.

- Create training programs to help parents understand gender issues and ways in which stereotyping, bias, discrimination, and subtle policies and practices can limit options for their children or young adults. Also teach them how to be change agents in schools and colleges.

Strategies in Counselor Education

One gender issue especially important in counselor education is that of incorporating new knowledge about women and men and new ways of knowing into training programs. The new theories of women's relational identity and self-in-relation are beginning to gain acceptance in counseling psychology. Qualitative research which complements empirical research and the logical positivist position is finding its way into professional counseling journals. "Agency-in-communion" is recognized as a goal for men as well as women. New knowledge in multicultural counseling is being integrated, where values of harmony, connectedness, wholeness, communal values, and subjective experience are more important than the Western values of fragmentation, autonomy, rationalism, and competition. Advocacy is needed for recognition of women as theorists and researchers in counseling psychology, along with multicultural theorists—and the new constructivist knowledge about gender and culture.

Conclusion

Gender-based advocacy, which focused heavily on educational equity for reducing violence against women in the last two decades, has made important strides. But the democratic goals of providing equal opportunity and equitable education for girls and boys still need attention, continuing old efforts but also adding new, with close attention to unfinished business for girls and women and new initiatives for boys and men. The new model for the "Multiple Dimensions of Identity" advanced by the Association for Multicultural Counseling and Development (AMCD) has helped us put some of the identity issues in perspective. The nine primary dimensions of identity include gender. We know that different dimensions may be important to a person at different stages of life. For example, in my own experience, in the high school years, social class was the major dimension, since we had little money and no expectation for me to go to college. As a beginning college professor, I became acutely aware of sexism in academe, and gender for the first time became more dominant. As I think now about a career transition, my identity as an older adult becomes more central.

For most persons of color, race and ethnicity are likely the most important dimension. The question should not be a competitive one of which identity is most important; rather, it should be, which of the multiple dimensions of identity is most important to this client, with this history, at this time, in this culture, and how does it affect her or his other identities and well-being? Those identities most associated with oppression, discrimination, and violence often will be the ones we emphasize. The need for counselor advocacy for gender-based issues remains because male-female relationship issues and violence and equity issues still need attention.

An ultimate ideal or goal for gender advocacy is to awaken "critical consciousness" of the importance and power of gender in one's life, of how it relates to and affects other identities, of how it interacts with the contextual and cultural issues, and through advocacy we can transform the organizations, institutions, and communities which perpetuate violent and inequitable treatment of human beings.

References and Resources

Hare-Mustin, R. & Marecek, J. (Eds.) (1990) . *Making a difference: Psychology and the construction of gender.* New Haven: Yale University Press.

Martell, N. (Ed.) (1998, September). Work it, Girl. George, 44.

Koerner, B.I. (1999, February 8). Where the boys aren't. *U.S. News and World Report, 47-55.*

Fogarty, B.E. (1998, October 3). More women on campus shouldn't be a concern. *Minneapolis Star Tribune,* A19.

Lee, V. E. (1997). Gender equity and the organization of schools, in *Gender, Equity, and Schooling* NY: Garland Publishing, Inc.

Bailey, S. (1992). *How schools shortchange girls.* Washington, D.C.: AAUW.

Hansen, L.S., Walker, J. & Flom, B. (1995). *GROWING SMART: What's working for girls in schools.* Washington, D.C.: AAUW.

American Institutes for Research. (1998). *Gender gaps: Where schools still fail our children.* Washington, D.C.: AAUW.

Hansen, L.S. (1997). *Integrative life planning: Critical tasks for career development and changing life patterns.* San Francisco: Jossey Bass.

Hansen, L.S. & Gama, E.P. (1996). Gender issues in multicultural counseling. In P. Pedersen, J.G. Draguns, W.J. Lonner, & J.E. Trimble (Eds.)*Counseling across cultures.* Thousand Oaks, CA: Sage.

Morrison, P. (1998). Where women are buried alive. Minneapolis Star Tribune, October, p. A11.

Convention on the Elimination of All Forms of Discrimination against Women. *Human Rights: A compilation of international instruments.* NY: United Nations, 1983.

Lee, C.C. (1989). Counseling Black adolescents: Critical roles and functions for counseling professionals. In. R. L. Jones (Ed.). *Black adolescents.* Berkeley, CA: Cobb & Henry.

Sanders, Jo. (1993). Computer Equity Expert Project. Final Report. NY: Center for Advanced Study in Education, CUNY Graduate Center.

Miller, J.B. & Stivers, I. P. (1997).*The healing connection: How women form relationships in therapy and in life.* Boston, MA: Beacon Press.

Arredondo, P., Toporek, R., Brown, S., Jones, J., Locke, D.C., Sanchez, J. & Stadler, H. (1996).*Operationalization of the multicultural counseling competencies.* Arlington, VA: Association for Multicultural Counseling and Development.

Additional Resources

WEEA Equity Resource Center, 55 Chapel Street, Newton, MA 02158—800-225-3088—email:weeapub@edc.org www.edc.org/WomensEquity

Wellesley College Centers for Research on Women, Wellesley, MA

National Council on Research on Women

Chapter Eleven

Domestic Violence: The Case for Social Advocacy

Mary Smith Arnold & Karen Sobieraj

"You Black, you pore, you ugly, you a woman, God
damn, he say, you ain't nothin at all."
— Alice Walker, *A Color Purple*

Counselors and other professionals who are concerned with
violence against women have strong and opposing convictions
about the causes and treatment of the violence (Gelles & Loseke,
1993). We believe that controversies over the genesis of violence
obscure the fact that women overwhelmingly experience violence
at the hands of their boyfriends, husbands, and other significant
men in their lives. Explanations of why domestic violence occurs,
whether it is due to psychopathology in the batterer, sociological
factors in the batterer's background, or even the web of patriarchal
values which structure society are all useless to the woman who
is victimized by someone she loves or once loved. In order to avoid
the obfuscation generated by divergent points of view on the
etiology of violence, we advocate that domestic violence be viewed
as a serious crime against the individual and society regardless of
its cause(es). The phenomenon of violence against women in this
society is as damaging to our national health as the wounds
perpetrators inflict on their victims.

The view that women "ain't nothin at all" is so prevalent in
our society that public sentiment has not challenged domestic
violence as intolerable social behavior. Many people think that
domestic violence is a natural outgrowth of intimate relationships.
The right of men to control their wives and girlfriends is widely
assumed in our society despite the economic and social gains made
by women within the last 30 years. Again noting the words of
Mr.__ in the novel *The Color Purple* by Alice Walker as he explains

to his son why he beats his wife, "Cause she my wife. Plus, she stubborn" (p.22). Mr.___, (fill in the name of the man you know who batters his wife or girlfriend) believes he is entitled to control his wife, his woman. Violence is rooted in disparities of power based on gender, race, class, sexual orientation, or interlocking combinations of these and other factors. Violence is an act which signifies domination and power over another person.

Although the term "domestic violence" is inclusive of psychological, emotional, and economic coercion (Walker, 1979), for purposes of this paper we will focus on physical assault and battery as the significant element. Therefore, we will use Kemp's (1998) definition of domestic violence as "A pattern of coercive behavior, which must include physical aggression or threat, commonly accompanied by other forms of controlling behaviors, that adults or adolescents use against their intimate partners" (p.226). Our focus on domestic violence is not to diminish the importance of ending all forms of violence but to reflect the urgency of the matter in relation to our work as counselors. The American Medical Association has stated that every five years the number of women killed due to family violence equals the number of Americans killed in the Vietnam War (Berry, 1995).

Domestic violence occurs across racial, ethnic, age, sexual orientation, religious, national origin, and socioeconomic lines. It eclipses all other forms of violence in the United States. Disenfranchised women who face other forms of vulnerability because of their sexual orientation, race, geographic location, immigrant status, or homelessness are just as likely to be victims of domestic violence as their more privileged sisters but they are less likely to report the abuse. Such women may also face the double jeopardy posed by maltreatment from institutions and social agencies, stemming from racism, heterosexism, classism, or xenophobia even as they struggle against their abusers.

We focus on domestic violence because it suggests that violence between intimates is still violence regardless of the gender configuration of the couple. More than 90% of reported cases of battering involve beating of women by men (Berry, 1995). Battering also occurs within same sex couples but it remains less visible because of the diminished status afforded these couples within our society. The portrayal of domestic violence as private violence or the personal acts between intimates serves as a barrier to fully eradicate this phenomenon. Somehow we accept that the physical assault of one's intimate partner is a lesser crime than assaulting a stranger on the street, leaving women and girls the most vulnerable population in society.

The following statistics reveal the prevalence and impact of domestic violence in our society:

- According to the most conservative estimate, each year 1 million women suffer nonfatal violence by an intimate.
- By other estimates, 4 million women experience a serious assault by an intimate partner during an average 12-month period.
- Each year, between 50,000 and 100,000 lesbian women and as many as 500,000 gay men are battered by their partner or former partner.
- Nearly 1 in 3 adult women experience at least one assault by a partner in adulthood.
- Eighty-eight percent of victims of domestic violence fatalities had a documented history of physical abuse by their abuser (www.abanet.org/domviol/stats.html).

These statistics represent a crisis in our society's ability to provide a nurturing environment. As counselors we recognize the devastating personal impact of violence on the victim's psychological, emotional, and physical health. As counselors we know that violence cannot be contained at one level of the family — that when a woman is victimized so are her children. As counselors we know that stopping the violence is an essential first step in the healing process for both the victim and the perpetrator.

Rationale

In order to more effectively serve our clients and contribute to creating an environment that is life enhancing for women and girls as well as for men and boys we must advocate an end to all violence against women. In a national study of women who escaped from battering, participants rated the effectiveness of formal help sources from very effective to somewhat effective. Results from the study reveal that participants selected women's groups (60 percent) and battered women's shelters (56 percent) as more effective than counseling or social services agencies (47 percent; Bowker, 1993). These figures indicate that we have much work to do if we are to effectively serve clients and help end the violence within society.

Our treatment of women who are in abusive relationships has located much of the cause and maintenance of the violence in individual women.Treatment concepts such as learned helplessness, Post Traumatic Stress Disorder, and even the notion of affiliation as the primary motivation in women, subtly suggest that fixing women will solve the problem. Although these perspectives on the effects of domestic violence on women have been groundbreaking in many respects, they may also prevent us from seeing and attending to the source of the problem: societal norms and gender socialization processes, disparities in power, and a society constructed to meet the needs of men at the expense of women.

A shift in our thinking as a profession about violence against women from individual victimization to viewing such violence as a symptom of societal ill health serves our clients and society better. Many have suggested that violence is a core element in the American consciousness and experience (Lee, 1998). A more accurate view is that violence is a core element in the social character of men, in contrast to women, in the United States (Stephenson, 1991). Placing the problem in its proper context allows us to address domestic and other forms of violence at its roots: societal values, norms, and institutions which encourage male violence. Lee (1998) stated, "[g]iven the continuing and insidious nature of violence in American society, professional counselors need to make further commitment to intervene not only on an interpersonal level but on a systemic level as well" (p.75). The need to work simultaneously at the interpersonal and systemic level with regard to victim and perpetrator issues is apparent. Challenging current social policies and practices which ultimately punish women for leaving or staying with their abuser would place professional counselors in a direct alliance with our clients which would strengthen our practice, empower clients, and contribute to reshaping the social context.

Social Advocacy Strategies

Ending violence against women requires fundamental social change in our gender relationships. However, to wait for such a thorough cultural transformation is to consign women to a perpetual state of victimization. What makes sense in responding to domestic violence is to activate our current criminal justice system to act in cases of domestic violence with the same conviction that it acts in cases of criminal assault and battery involving strangers. Domestic violence is a crime which calls for stiffer penalties and stronger enforcement of current laws. In every state we have laws which cover battery, assault, harassment, and murder. However, in many states domestic violence is a misdemeanor rather than a felony (Felder & Victor, 1996). The following measures are directed at igniting the criminal justice system to serve and protect women and children:

- Advocate that the laws and penalties which apply to physical assault and battery be applied to assailants in domestic violence cases.
- Advocate against "dual arrests" and other measures which punish women for defending themselves against their assailants.
- Call for "must-arrest" legislation in your state or county in domestic violence cases; if they have it, support a group which monitors its enforcement.
- Encourage the courts to support treatment programs for first time offenders that are linked to sentencing as an alternative to incarceration as well as parole and probation.
- Work with interdisciplinary teams to establish written protocols, policies, and procedures for law enforcement personnel, prosecutors, and courts that are sensitive to victims.
- Publish and widely post flyers listing the legal rights of victims of an assault and battery and the penalties.
- Monitor and support law enforcement officials in order to discourage differential enforcement based on race, class, or sexual orientation.

The above strategies are directed at the legal system because we must become more effective at forcing the system to serve and protect women and children. The police, courts, and our legal statutes are the first line of defense for women who have been assaulted.

Client Advocacy

Counselors bring important strengths to social advocacy efforts: knowledge of common problems faced by clients and a set of interpersonal skills useful to community building (Lewis & Arnold, 1998). Counselors working within the principles of interdisciplinary collaboration (Bemak, 1998) can promote social change through the following strategies:

- Contact the National Council of Juvenile and Family Court Judges for their recommendations and model proposals for creating a state or county multidisciplinary and multi-systems family violence coordinating councils.

a) Lobby local judges and victim advocates to establish a family violence coordinating council comprised of decision makers and stakeholders from public, not-for-profit, and private sectors that are involved with victims, perpetrators, and children and related issues of family violence.

b) Partner with women's shelters and victim advocacy groups to provide cross-training programs for staff members, trainees, and most of all ourselves.

c) Partner with women's shelters and those who work with perpetrators to develop intervention strategies, coordinate services, and create integrated therapeutic treatment plans to be used, when appropriate, with couples and families.

d) Advocate that risk assessments for violent behavior be a standard element of all protocols for child custody cases and supervised visitation.

- Utilize public health strategies to alter the public perception that domestic violence, and violence against women in general, is an individual or familial disorder. This would include the use of public health strategies to promulgate that:

a) Domestic violence is as unacceptable as violence toward strangers and that it equally violates the law and society's standards for the health and well being of its members.

b) Women and children are victimized by the abuser and that they never court, "ask for it" or "deserve it" as a rational consequence.

c) Non-violent individuals, families, and communities promote the general prosperity and well-being of the society and reflect the standard of acceptable behavior.

d) It is the role and responsibility of all community members to insure the physical safety and freedom of vulnerable or dependent members of the community.

e) Ensure that print, visual, and electronic media accurately portray the message that violence against women occurs across all groups and strata of our society; and that they present domestic violence as a societal problem rather than a symptom of distressed environments, substance abuse, poverty, lack of education, or ethnically determined behavior.

- Monitor and lobby print, advertising, and entertainment media to increase use of cooperative, symbiotic, and equitable images of men and women rather than promoting predator-prey relationships. Strategies would include:

    a) Write, call, or e-mail media executives when unacceptable images or themes are used in advertising, music, television, movies, and other forms of entertainment. Also, indicate your approval when appropriate.

    b) Campaign against products which promote sexualized violence and brutality against women.

    c) Boycott products or promotions which continue to demean the status or role of women or glorify predator-prey relationships.

    d) Actively support and organize efforts to highlight products and promotions which reflect equitable, symbiotic, non-violent male-female interactions.

- Include in your presentations, training workshops, and consultations accurate information regarding the etiology, assessment, intervention, and advocacy measures useful in prevention, early intervention, and treatment of the batterer and support for victims of abuse. This would include:

    a) Teaching clients, students, and social service personnel how to remove barriers to seeking help in domestic violence cases.

    b) Teaching intervention approaches which do not blame or further victimize women for the violence directed at them. This would include the elimination of the "all-or-nothing, leave him-or-suffer" tone which subtly place the responsibility for stopping or the continuing abuse on women rather than their abusers.

    c) Use treatment approaches which are culturally sensitive; value client self-determination; are problem solving oriented; assess the client's resources; and start where the client is affectively and behaviorally.

    d) Develop and teach interventions and techniques designed to assist perpetrators in taking responsibility for their actions and to learn non-violent means of interactions.

e) Include assessment of domestic violence as a "Standard of Care" for all medical and mental health providers at multiple stages during the service process.

- Encourage, participate, and conduct outcome-based research on prevention programs, treatment interventions, impact of incarceration, help-seeking behaviors of victims, and response behaviors, attitudes, and skill utilization of law officials, medical and social service personnel, judicial systems and, most importantly, counselors.

  a) Apply for grant funds through state and federal agencies such as the Department of Justice to improve training in the assessment, intervention, and referral of victims of domestic violence.

Legislative Advocacy

- Call your congressional representatives and lobby for the reauthorization of crucial components of the 1994 Violence Against Women Act for inclusion in the 1999 legislation to combat violence against women before the 106th Congress. Funds for the National Domestic Violence Hotline were eliminated as well as important funding for grants in the areas of prevention, education, and research. Demand that these measures be reinstated.

  a) Work with the ACA Public Policy and Legislation Committee to continue advocating for effective legislation to combat violence against women.

Conclusion

We offer a note of caution; as we write this paper new evidence is emerging regarding racial bias in the arrest and prosecution of men of color (*The Chicago Tribune*, January 10, 1999, A-1). Advocacy efforts would have to include an awareness of such bias as well as measures to guard against differential enforcement of laws. Privileged men are no more entitled to exercise violence against women than men of color or poor and working class men. Domestic violence must not become just another means to unfairly arrest and incarcerate innocent men of color thereby avoiding addressing the problem of violence at the systemic level in society.

Against the backdrop of the above caveat, great strides have occurred over the last 20 years in combating domestic violence due to the efforts of activists, practitioners, scholars, law enforcement, and judicial personnel. It is precisely because of these gains that it has become obvious that a shift in our thinking and our approach to this issue is necessary. We have yet to stem the tide of violence against women despite the collective efforts of legions of helping professionals. Eradicating domestic violence requires a broad societal consensus that violence against women is offensive to our national character. Counselors can help build that consensus.

References

Berry, D. B. (1995). *The domestic violence source book: Everything you need to know*. Chicago: Contemporary Books.

Bowker, L. H. (1993). A battered woman's problems are social not psychological. In R. J. Gelles, & D. R. Loseke (Eds.), *Current controversies on family violence*. (pp. 154-170). Newbury Park, CA: Sage Publications.

Felder, R. L., & Victor, B. (1995). *Getting away with murder: Weapons for the war against domestic violence*. New York: Simon & Schuster.

Gelles, R. J., & Loseke, D. R. (1993). *Current controversies on family violence*. Newbury Park, CA: Sage Publications.

Kemp, A. (1998). *Abuse in the family: An introduction*. Pacific Grove, CA: Brooks/Cole.

Lee, C. C., & Brydes, J. L. (1998). Challenging interpersonal violence. In C. C. Lee & G. R. Walz (Eds.). *Social action: A mandate for counselors*. Alexandria, VA: American Counseling Association and ERIC Counseling and Student Services Clearinghouse.

Lewis, J. A., & Marnold, M. S. (1998). From Multiculturalism to social action. In C. C. Lee & G. R. Walz (Eds.). *Social action: A mandate for counselors*. Alexandria, VA: American Counseling Association and ERIC Counseling and Student Services Clearinghouse.

Stephenson, J. (1991). *Men are not cost-effective: Male crime in America*. Napa, CA: Diemer, Smith Publishing Company, Inc.

Walker, A. (1982). *The color purple*. New York: Harcourt Brace Jovanovich, Publishers.

Walker, L. E. (1979). *The battered woman*. New York: Harper Perennial

Recommended Readings

The Domestic Violence Source Book by Dawn Bradley Berry, Contemporary Books, 1995

Getting Away with Murder: Weapons for the War Against Domestic Violence, editors: Raoul Felder and Barbara Victor, Simon & Schuster, 1996

Violence Against Women: Philosophical Perspectives, editors: Stanley G. French, Wanda Teays, & Laura M. Purdy, Cornell University Press, 1998

Defending Our Lives by Susan Murphy-Milano, Doubleday, 1996

Websites - Organizations - Hotlines

American Bar Association
Commission on Domestic Violence
740 15th Street, NW 9th Floor
Washington, DC 20005-1022
e-mail: abacdv@abanet.org
Internet address: www.abanet.org/domviol/home.html/

Advocates for Abused and Battered Lesbians
P.O. Box 85596
Seattle, WA 98105-9998
e-mail: support@aabl.org
Internet address: www.aabl.org/
(This is not a national organization but it provides information about services in other parts of the country.)

Family Violence Prevention Fund
383 Rhode Island Street, Suite #304

San Francisco, CA 94103-5133
e-mail: fund@igc.apc.org
Internet address: www.igc.org/fund/

National Coalition Against Domestic Violence (NCADV)
P.O. Box 18749
Denver, CO 80218
Phone (303) 839-1852
Internet address: www.ncadv.org
NCADV - Public Policy Office
119 Constitution Avenue, NE
Washington, DC 20002
Phone (202) 544-7358 Fax (202) 544-7893

National Domestic Violence Hotline
1-800-799-7233 (SAFE)
TDD for the hearing impaired
1-800-787-3224

National Organization for Women (NOW)
P.O. Box 96824
Washington, DC 20090-6824
e-mail: now@now.org
Internet address: www.now.org/

NOW - Action Center
1000 16th Street, NW Suite 700
Washington, DC 20036
Phone: (202) 331-006 FAX (202) 785-8576
TTY: (202) 331-9002

Mary Smith Arnold is a professor in the psychology and counseling department at Governors State University in University Park, Ill. Karen Sobieraj is a professor of social work at Governors State University in University Park, Ill.

Chapter Twelve

Advocacy on Issues Related to Addictions

Michael J. Taleff

Advocating for a population with an addictive disorder holds extraordinary challenges, but it also offers extraordinary rewards. The challenge is to embrace a cause with which most people in this country hold little sympathy. The primary reward is that once advocating has begun, it can help ignite an addicted person's self-respect. And if a single flame of self-respect can begin, think of the bonfire that thousands if not millions of people could collectively display.

This paper will outline some of the salient problems associated with advocating for addictive populations, summarize ideas for general advocating, and identify organizations that are currently involved in advocacy. This short piece will close with a dream of what the end product or goal of successful advocacy might be.

Before we begin this little journey, let us get the definition straight. Advocacy refers to the action of the person or organization that pleads, recommends, or supports an argument, cause or policy. For our purpose, advocacy defends or stands up for the rights of a person with an addictive problem. There are elements of counseling, politics, and passion to be seen within the advocacy process. All contribute toward changing things for the better.

Challenge of Addiction Advocacy

Perhaps the critical question of advocacy for addictive populations is why we should put forth the effort on behalf of such a group. Many would argue that it doesn't make sense to advocate for people who seemingly bring on the problem by their own behavior. Various people would still claim that addicts willfully contribute to the situations in which they find themselves. "I mean, don't addicts have to stop whatever they are doing and go out of their way to seek and eventually use chemicals?" This type of logic suggests that in order to get worse the addict has to do something that looks a lot like willfulness to advance the progression of the problem. It isn't like Parkinson's Disease that progresses without active promotion. What about the crack addict mother who abandons her children for days in squalor so she can "cop" and repeatedly use? What about the adolescent who at age 13 or 14 begins to prostitute himself or herself to get drugs? How do you advocate for them? Think about the pushers and users who not only sell drugs to the mother and adolescent but are out of control themselves. How does one advocate for them? It is difficult to plead for money and policy changes for Uncle Fred who has smoked most of his life and now has a major lung problem. It is equally difficult to advocate for Aunt Emma who has been obese all her life, and now has diabetic as well as cardiac complications.

Moreover, this situation is complicated by the fact that the government indirectly contributes to the stigma problem. When a regime declares war on a segment of its people or calls for "a crusade to wipe out this plague," its statements elicit moral overtones. It is these moral overtones that add to the ever present "disgrace" of addiction.

With any of the appetite or excessive disorders, there are tremendous stigmas to overcome. We just don't see telethons set up to raise money for addictions research. It is not a big draw for charity work. Most people with an addiction are viewed as second-class citizens and as morally inferior. Although some progress has been made to see these problems as diseases, the stigma remains very strong for the majority of the public and even among state and national representatives and policy makers.

Then why do it? Why advocate for these people? The answer is deceptively simple. We advocate because, despite the problem, they are people. They happen to be caught up in a terrible situation. A real ray of hope on the horizon drives this point home. It is that explanations about addiction are improving from generation to generation. Each level of improvement is based on scientific thought and evidence. As this scientific base builds, it steps further away from the age-old stigma that dogs this problem. Science and stigma cannot coexist. Thus, another reason for advocating is that it will assist in finding solid answers for the dynamics of addiction. But, we need the research money and a collective will to accomplish this enormous task. We also need a dream akin to walking on the moon. Advocacy has the potential to realize all of this.

Addiction Advocacy Strategies

Going back to our definition, to advocate means to plead, recommend, and support an argument, cause, or policy. In our case, we are advocating for all people with an addiction in order to support their rights and challenging the stigma and discrimination associated with the problem. This can be done on a number of levels. One is the personal, another is within a group, and the third is a combination of both.

It seems fitting that any movement toward advocacy begins somewhere within the person. We usually need some inner feeling of outrage to provoke motivation, which in turn stimulates action. That activated person then contacts someone else who becomes caught up in the movement, and then they capture a third, fourth, and so forth. Following this, more formal groups are created. When they develop a certain level of respect and credence, these groups can lobby and bring pressure to bear on those who can help make a change. If many people work together to make a change, it is more likely to happen than if one person tries it alone. This is the case for addiction advocacy.

In Pennsylvania, as in other states, this general scenario began a number of years ago with an organization entitled The Drug and Alcohol Services Providers of PA. This was and remains a public policy advocacy group. Recently, Promoting Recovery Organizations-Achieving Community Togetherness (PRO-ACT) began to organize the recovery community to promote pride and dignity in recovery, as well as promoting a positive, distinct community identity. Two grants were awarded by the Center for Substance Abuse Treatment (CSAT) to Pennsylvania. The first is The Statewide Pro Alliance, and the local version entitled The Bucks County Council on Alcoholism and Drug Dependence. General objectives of the latter include reducing the stigma of addiction, having volunteers give back to the community, focusing on drug- and alcohol-free social events, participating in evaluating treatment services, and educating the recovering consumer in regard to legislation and public policy.

A little known aspect of advocacy is that it has the potential to change situation variables that often account for addictive disorders, such as a poor environment, housing, and education. Advocated money directed at these variables may have tremendous effects on an addiction, versus resorting to the worn-out cliché that the client is in some form of denial. In fact, a sub-unit within clinical settings could be arranged to advocate for better housing, a safe environment, and a quality education.

However, this advocating process need not be limited to the recovering person. Such a process can support addiction counselors, prevention specialists, and supervisors. Often, these dedicated individuals fail to receive the respect they deserve because of the clientele they serve.

This whole process can be viewed as a benevolent snowball rolling down a hill and gaining more momentum as it moves. This is where the visualized dream plays a pivotal role. Imagine a diverse crowd of 500,000 people, recovering from various addictions, on the mall in Washington, D.C. openly advocating for their rights and dignity. They come from all over the country and shout in unison "Increase knowledge, stop the stigma." That turnout and petition then reverberates down the halls of congress and the White House, and soon people in power start to listen, understand, and direct money and personnel to really address this problem. But, the outcome of this work is the best part of the dream. Just a few short years later, average people sitting in their living rooms watching TV no longer look down their noses at the someone with an addiction, nor view them as sinners. Because of the answers obtained by the advocated research and educational outreach programs, the public understands. They do this because of the results brought about by the hard work and sweat involved in advocacy. In our dream, that work has finally put an end to the stigma and shame of addiction.

Suggested Resources

National Alliance for Model State Drug Laws
333 N. Fairfax St., Suite 201
Alexandra, VA 22314
703-863-6100
www.natalliance.org/main.html
(This organization has developed model state laws and discriminated information across the country.)

National Coalition of State Alcohol & Drug Treatment and Prevention Associations
c/o Legal Action
236 Massachusetts Ave. N.E., Suite 505
Washington, DC 20002
202-544-5478
(A national public policy advocacy group.)

National Council on Alcoholism and Drug Dependence, Inc.
(NCADD)
12 W 21 Street
New York, NY 10010
(212) 206-6770
www.ncadd.org
(NCADD sponsors the Registry of Addiction Recovery (ROAR), a national volunteer campaign to fight the stigma associated with addiction.)

Alcohol Policies Project
Center for Science in the Public Interest
1875 Connecticut Ave. N.W. Suite 300
Washington, DC 20009-5728
(202) 332-9110 x 385
www.cspinst.org/booze/
(The Alcohol Polices Project is a watchdog group that offers advocacy and information on federal and state policy.)

Center for Alcohol Advertising
2140 Shattuck Ave. Suite 1110
Berkeley, CA. 94704
(510) 649-8942
www.traumafdn,org/alcohol/ads/index.html
(The Center monitors alcohol promotion and advertising and offers assistance with media advocacy.)

The International Coalition of Addiction Studies Education
(INCASE)
www.homestead.com/INCASE/index.html
(INCASE is an organization of substance abuse educators dedicated to scholarship addictions studies instruction, training, as well as promoting research, especially at the post secondary level.)

Join Together
441 Stuart St., 7th Floor
Boston, MA 02116
(617) 437-1500
www.jointogether.org
(This is a national resource helping communities fight substance abuse and gun violence. It provides access to the latest news and research on substance abuse and gun violence.)

Legal Action Center
236 Massachusetts Ave. N.E., Suite 505
Washington, DC 20002
www.lac.org
(The Legal Action Center provides advocacy for expanding addiction treatment and prevention. It fights discrimination against people who are in recovery from various addictions and HIV/AIDS.)

Mothers Against Drunk Driving (MADD)
511 E. John Carpenter Freeway, Suite 700
Irving, TX 75062
(214) 744-6233
www.madd.org
(MADD is a nonprofit organization that focuses on effective solutions to drunk driving and underage drinking problems, while supporting the victims of drunk driving.)

National Association of Alcohol and Drug Counselors (NAADAC)
1119 North Fort Myer Drive, Suite 900
Arlington, VA 22209
(NAADAC is the national professional chemical dependency organization for counselors, educators, administrators, and other health givers. It also tracks legislative actions and advocates for policy change.)

National Association for Children of Alcoholics (NACOA)
11426 Rockville, MD 20875
(301) 468-0985
www.health.org.nacoa
(NACOA advocates for children and families affected by chemical dependencies.)

Physician Leadership for National Drug Policy
Center for Alcohol and Addiction Studies
Brown University
Providence, RI 02912
(401) 444-1818
center.butler.brown.edu/plndp/
(The Leadership is a group of physicians who advocate for effective policies on addiction treatment.)

Michael J. Taleff is an assistant professor at Penn State University. He is the project director of chemical dependency programs in the counselor education department and president of the International Coalition of Addiction Studies Education.

Chapter Thirteen

Advocacy for People with HIV/AIDS

John Cebuhar

I have been intimately involved with HIV/AIDS since 1988, when I began counseling heroin addicts in a methadone maintenance setting in Chicago. I, myself, have lived with HIV infection since my own diagnosis in 1989. I share this with you so that you will know that I have had to become a strong advocate for myself as well as for others. My own diagnosis and my work with hundreds of People with HIV and AIDS have markedly changed both my counseling style and my philosophy regarding advocacy.

Background

The first cases of Acquired Immune Deficiency Syndrome (AIDS) were reported by a Los Angeles physician in 1981, when he noted a specific and deadly form of pneumonia that soon proved fatal to the two young, homosexual males who had been infected. In 1981, the mortality rate for AIDS from time of infection until death was approximately 20 months, with major incapacitation and debilitation present from early in the onset of the disease. Methods for detection of the HIV virus were not available until 1985. The first effective medication, Retrovir (AZT), was introduced in 1986. Newer classes of drugs were introduced in 1995 and 1996. When the "AIDS Drug Cocktail" was introduced in 1996, the Centers for Disease Control and Prevention noted a marked decline in the mortality rate from HIV infection. The drug cocktail is a combination of one or more drugs from at least two of the three classes of drugs that work in different ways to inhibit the reproduction of HIV. The new drug combinations do not afford a cure, nor are the combinations effective across the entire spectrum of HIV-infected individuals. This spectrum has broadened beyond men who have unprotected sex with men, injection drug users and their partners, and offspring born to HIV-infected mothers. HIV infection has spread to the heterosexual population at an alarming rate, especially in communities of color such as the African-American and Hispanic populations. AIDS remains a leading cause of death among adolescents and young adults.

Successful eradication of AIDS has yet to be realized, but the disease is now considered by many virologists to be difficult to control but controllable, at least for the present time. How long the new classes of drugs will remain effective is not known. What is known is that HIV is able to mutate to new strains rapidly, that the new drugs do not work with all people, and that both the drug side-effects and the dosing schedule can often lead to treatment failure. Prevention of HIV infection through abstinence or safer sexual and drug use practice remains an integral aspect of disease containment.

No cure for HIV/AIDS exists, and a cure may never be realized. Medical experts have switched from a strategy of developing a "magic bullet" to kill the retrovirus to developing a variety of different classes of drugs that act on different parts of the retrovirus in order to inhibit viral reproduction. Pharmacologists have also worked on developing medications that can effectively combat the myriad of diseases that can attack the body once immune-compromise has been realized. Diseases associated with AIDS include leukemia; cancers; tuberculosis (both pulmonary and organ and bone related varieties); Cytomegalovirus, which destroys eyesight; pneumonia and other respiratory illnesses; wasting syndrome; muscle-mass loss; dementia; neuropathy and other neural damage such as epilepsy and other seizure disorders; severe fatigue; depression; anorexia; heart, liver, and kidney disease and failure; anemia; and memory and motor-function problems brought about by organisms that attack the brain. AIDS medical experts are attempting to develop methods to rebuild the immune system that has been partially destroyed or completely impacted by HIV infection. Finally, the medical and pharmaceutical communities must develop new medications to combat the myriad side-effects associated with the medications taken to combat the primary infection of HIV. The side effects of the drugs can be as trying and difficult to manage as the disease itself.

Counseling People with AIDS

When I first began my work with People with AIDS, I had the mistaken concept that my counseling approach would closely follow models developed for death and dying. I quickly learned, however, that this would not be the driving force of my practice. I now offer a new term for my counseling practice with People with AIDS: revitalization counseling. That is, counseling that brings new life to an individual.

The tasks of the client who is infected with HIV continue to be life tasks, and it is only through successful realization of these life tasks that a client can, when he or she chooses and if and when it is appropriate, initiate life-closure processes. If you are a counselor who wishes to work with People with AIDS or other life-threatening illnesses, you should put away your books on death and dying, estate planning, medical powers-of-attorney and medical directives. Reach instead for life-affirming, motivational methods that can help your clients reach their goals. Your clients, like all of us, will continue to have goals until they no longer live. The listening skills that you have honed through practice will serve as an excellent basis for counseling because they will enable your clients to teach you what it is like to live with a catastrophic illness and potential death. Someday, you too will need this learning for your own developmental process of living and dying. This process of discovery can be enlightening and exciting for you as a counselor, as well as for your clients. Your connection with your clients will also increase your awareness that advocacy skills need to be part of your repertoire.

The Need for Advocacy

Our social service systems and entitlement programs are bureaucratic, difficult to access, and not designed to handle the needs of the terminally ill. Social Security Disability or Supplemental Security Income can take years to access. Housing entitlement programs such as Section 8 have waiting lists of up to ten years. Pharmaceutical assistance programs to pay for basic medications for AIDS (which can run as high as $2,000-$3,000 per month) have spending caps and are often closed. Food stamp assistance is available to only the most indigent. Public Assistance is a nightmare and requires a total spend-down of all assets before any entitlement. Assisted living programs for People with AIDS have waiting lists. People who have a history of substance abuse may be denied services until they have two years of sobriety. All too often, people with AIDS become homeless and join our other unintitled, faceless, thrown-away citizens who must scurry to survive. Then, accessing services becomes even more difficult because the individual has no permanent address. The client now has no way to maintain regular hygiene and no assistance with a difficult drug regimen of pills every eight hours. The individual's medications may be stolen, confiscated, or simply lost as he or she struggles to survive.

AIDS stigmatizes. AIDS discrimination exists in housing, in employment, in social-service access, in medical care, and in the very fabric of a society that chooses to blame the individual for his or her illness. Just at the time when the individual is most in need of nurturing and solace, it is ripped away. He or she is sent out of the community as a shunned individual to face life alone. If the client at this stage adapts or reverts to coping mechanisms such as drugs and alcohol, we use that as further proof of the righteousness of our inhumanity.

The Americans With Disabilities Act should serve as a framework for all of our talented individuals who, regardless of their physical or mental affliction, have a right to employment that will utilize their talents. We know that we are not all created equal in our talents and abilities and we know that we do not always stay equal in our ability to perform our work in a uniform manner. We also know, however, that each of us has some special gift or talent that is needed by our society. Providing for reasonable accommodations for those with special needs gives us the privilege of sharing in the talents of these people. Both sides benefit from this equation, as people are returned to situations in which they can be fruitful and productive members of society.

Although the federal government has passed the Americans With Disabilities Act (ADA), employment discrimination continues to exist. The ADA was rather vague in its intent and the real law is being litigated through court action. The agency charged with handling ADA complaints, the Equal Employment Opportunity Commission, has been downsized and already must handle all racial, age and other discrimination matters under other federal civil rights legislation. A complaint can take as long as two years, at which time a client is then given a right to sue letter and must pursue his or her case through federal court at his or her own expense. Because of Washington politics, the federal court has suffered a severe shortage of judicial appointments and thus a case can linger in the courts for years. Bear in mind that your elected officials have created this backlog and that the wronged party may not live to see justice!

Local, state, and federal governments all play roles in these problems. State governments throughout the United States have adapted a strategy of shifting the poor onto Medicaid in order to shift the balance of payment to the federal government. Social service programs funded on a state level are being downsized or closed, but the federal government is resistant to sharing the burden of payment. While this war between the states and the federal government is waged, your clients suffer from lack of entitlement and from bureaucratic mismanagement. Where can they turn but to you? You must become their voice!

Personal Experiences with Advocacy

When I began providing services to People with AIDS, I learned immediately I would have to serve as an advocate for clients having difficulties with social service entitlements. One of the first issues I dealt with was the time frame for Social Security benefits. Some of my clients had to wait as long as three years from the date of application until benefits were awarded. Often, the client did not live long enough to realize his or her benefits. I knew that this was an injustice and wrote to my senator, Paul Simon, who was running for President at the time. The Senator agreed with me and forwarded my letter to the Director of Social Security, who also agreed. The system was changed. A position of ombudsman was created within the Social Security Administration and Social Security began a process of educating case managers about the nuances of the system.

My clients also had difficulties accessing basic health care. For instance, a major drug store chain in Chicago was offering flu-shots as a service to customers but refusing shots if an individual reported to the attending nurse that he or she was HIV-positive. I was asked to be a tester, that is, to go to one of the stores, report my HIV status, be refused services, and serve as a witness in litigation. I chose to call the chairman of the drug store chain and educate him about why this practice was discriminatory and would lead to a law suit and adverse publicity. The practice was changed within twenty-four hours.

As these kinds of situations have arisen over the years, I have become more and more comfortable with my advocacy role. I was intimidated the first time I called a congressional office, but I was surprised to find that the staff was open, friendly, and interested in helping. As I communicated with the staffs of elected officials, I was able to see that education was a two-way street. Elected officials who had been educated about the special needs of citizens could raise relevant issues during budget hearings. I was also educated in turn by the staffs of elected officials so that I became more knowledgeable about the laws. As my own knowledge of the system grew, I was able to be more effective in providing accurate information to the client about possible pitfalls on the way to achieving entitlements. At the same time, I became more confident in dealing with applicable agencies. As my networking developed, I was able to streamline my advocacy by knowing who in an applicable office was most open to providing accurate information and direct assistance. I learned about the constituent services provided by members of congress and about the speed with which a letter to the appropriate representative or administrator can move the process along. I learned that, when my requests were initially denied, I could seek out additional information and develop a new action strategy.

Conclusion

Let me share with you the definition of discrimination that I have developed over the years that I have been privileged to work with People with AIDS. Discrimination is to do nothing when you can do something. Nothing versus something! What might something involve?
- Initiating a telephone call or a letter
- Providing an empathic ear
- Getting angry at injustice
- Fighting our own complacency
- Adding our voice
- Taking a client to an entitlement hearing
- Educating ourselves
- Becoming teachable by allowing our clients to teach
- Accepting the role of advocate as a central focus of our work

Advocacy serves as an effective manner in which to clear the board of solvable external problems so that effective counseling can begin. Advocacy clearly and strongly establishes our credentials as effective counselors, engages the client, and fosters a bond. Through advocacy, we help our current clients, empower these clients to help themselves and others, and thus enhance our effectiveness as practitioners and human beings.

John Cebuhar is an AIDS advocate in Chicago, Ill.

Chapter Fourteen

Working with Mental Health Advocacy Groups

Megan Tenety & Mark Kiselica

With the downsizing of state-run psychiatric institutions and better psychotropic medication, an increasing number of mentally ill persons are returning to the community. At the same time, limited community resources and constraints imposed by managed care organizations are limiting the quality and quantity of services provided to the mentally ill. Therefore, counselors must develop creative strategies for meeting the needs of their mentally ill clients. This theme paper describes how counselors can access and use advocacy groups, whose services are typically provided free of charge, to assist their mentally ill clients.

Advocacy groups are a diverse collection of organizations, people, and agendas. Although many advocacy groups join together to work in coalitions or meet common goals, they do not always act as a united front. The agendas and tactics of groups vary as do the members, attenders, and the issues they serve. Some advocacy groups have substantial political respect, while others are considered more radical, taking extreme stances on issues such as opposition to psychiatry or the nature of mental illnesses.

The make-up of organizations also varies. Some organizations are run by "consumers" (i.e., individuals who utilize the mental health system) who may be supportive of the mental health system. Other organizations are run by individuals who call themselves "psychiatric survivors." Generally, psychiatric survivors reject the system and oppose forced treatment laws and the use of psychotropic medications. Some organizations are solely run by the individuals they serve, some mandate a ratio of consumers and non-consumers, and others do not include consumers. Different organizations often represent the interest of contrasting parties in the mental health care debate—psychiatrists, consumers, families, civil libertarians, politicians, managed care providers, and psychologists.

The diversity within advocacy groups has caused some debate and conflict among them. According to Paul R. Benson in a 1992 article in the *International Journal of Law and Psychiatry*, the discrepancy between various groups serves to weaken the possible impact advocacy groups could have in the political arena. Despite this, the presence of advocacy groups is believed to be a major force behind the improved services offered to the mentally ill.

Rationale

There are many factors behind the growing advocacy movement for mentally ill individuals. These factors include the prevalence of mental illness in society, deinstitutionalization, the restrictions of managed care, an increased awareness of the rights of the mentally ill, and empowerment of mentally ill clients. Despite the growing importance of advocacy groups, information regarding who they are, what they do, and how to access them is not readily available. This article is designed to provide counselors with this information.

Strategies

Advocacy groups provide a wide range of services for consumers, family members, and professionals. In addition to offering direct services and support groups, advocacy groups work to:

- Enhance the rights of persons diagnosed with mental illnesses
- Educate consumers, the public, and professionals
- Maintain toll-free hotlines and act as referral sources
- Lobby state and federal governments on behalf of the mentally ill
- Assess the level of care offered by mental health facilities
- Empower consumers
- Advocate for increased research funding
- Facilitate workshops and annual conferences
- Advocate for improved community resources (housing, job training, etc.)
- Decrease the stigmatization of mental illness
- Defend the civil rights of people with mental illnesses
- Offer support groups for the mentally ill and their families

Advocacy groups provide counselors with a powerful and valuable resource. Counselors can access advocacy groups to locate other resources and information or to gain the support of a larger voice in an effort to advocate for a client. Counselors can enhance the range of services offered to clients and their families by linking them with advocacy groups. Through advocacy groups, clients and their family members can share experiences, information, and support with others in similar situations, thereby connecting them with a larger community and decreasing their feelings of isolation and stigmatization. Advocacy groups are a service that clients can use themselves to feel empowered, to learn more about issues that affect them, and to have a say on such issues.

Suggested Resources

Today, there are hundreds of advocacy groups working to improve the lives of the mentally ill. The following list is provided as a quick reference to some of the largest advocacy groups currently in existence.

National Mental Health Association (NMHA). Founded in 1909 by Clifford Beers under its original name, The American Foundation for Mental Hygiene, NMHA is a mental health consumer advocacy organization devoted to fighting mental illnesses and promoting mental health. NMHA advocates for increased research funding, supports community mental health center programs, and assesses the level of care in residential facilities. This organization also works to promote the growth of consumer self-help groups. NMHA lobbies for more humane treatment of the mentally ill and for expanded services in the community. This organization was a major force behind the Mental Health Act of 1946 and the Community Mental Health Centers Act of 1963. NMHA serves as a national resource for educational materials, conducts public education, and works to increase public action through the media.

NMHA can be contacted at: NMHA 1021 Prince Street, Alexandria, VA 22314-2971, Phone: 703.684.7722, 800.969.NMHA, Web: www.nmha.org.

National Alliance for the Mentally Ill (NAMI). Founded in 1979, NAMI was created to address the host of problems resulting from the deinstitutionalization movement. NAMI began when a number of local self-help groups for families of the mentally ill discovered each other's existence and joined together. NAMI has become a nationwide network of local and state affiliates. NAMI offers a variety of services for persons with mental illnesses and their families, such as self-help programs, public awareness, encouraging cooperative dialogue between service providers, direct services to consumers, response to families in pain, and pursuit of increased research funding. NAMI targets outreach efforts for special groups, such as mental health consumers, minorities, siblings of mentally ill persons, families affected by a member's mental illness, families of mentally ill chemical abusers, and families caught in the criminal justice system. NAMI is a consumer organization that works in coalition with professional and provider organizations.

NAMI can be contacted at: NAMI, 200 N. Glebe Road, Suite 1015, Arlington, VA 22203-3754, Phone: 703.524.7600, 800.950.NAMI, TDD: 703.516.7991, Web: www.nami.org.

National Empowerment Center (NEC). The NEC is a consumer-run organization that works to carry a message of recovery, empowerment, hope, and healing to people with mental illnesses. The NEC offers a national directory of mutual support groups, drop-in centers and state-wide organizations, networking and coalition building, a collection of free or low priced materials, education and training to providers from a consumer/survivor perspective, and a database with hundreds of topics of interest.

NEC can be contacted at: NEC, 20 Ballard Road, Lawrence, MA 01843-1018, Phone: 800.769.3728, Web: www.power2u.org.

Bazelon Center for Mental Health Law. Formerly know as the Mental Health Law Project, Bazelon is a non-profit public interest group concerned with promoting the civil rights of people with mental illnesses and developmental disabilities. The Bazelon Center advocates for mental health policies at the federal and state levels; monitors issues; provides technical assistance; advocates for the Supplemental Security Income program, protection, and advocacy groups; outreach programs; and programs serving infants and children. The Bazelon Center is a partnership of lawyers, policy advocates, mental health experts, and mental health consumers. Bazelon Center attorneys provide legal advocacy for the civil rights and human dignity of people with mental disabilities. Please note that the Bazelon Center is not able to handle individual requests for information or assistance. The Center's website does provide links to other advocacy resources that can offer assistance to persons with mental or developmental disabilities.

The Bazelon Center can be contacted at: Bazelon Center, 1101 15th Street NW, Washington, DC 20005, Phone: 202.467.5730, Web: www.bazelon.org.

National Association For Rights Protection And Advocacy

(NARPA). NARPA claims to be the only independent advocacy organization in the United States. Formed in 1980, NARPA is dedicated to promoting policies and strategies that represent the preferred options of people who are labeled as mentally disabled. The central issues of concern to NARPA are the abolition of all forced treatment laws, opposition to electroconvulsive therapy, and the enhancement of community services.

NARPA can be contacted at: NARPA, 587 Marshall, St. Paul, MN 55102, Phone: 612.224.7761, Web: www.connix.com/~narpa.

Finding Other Resources

The advocacy groups described above may not meet the unique needs of an individual consumer or professional. Many other advocacy groups exist, including the following: National Depressive and Manic Depressive Association; MADNESS; National Alliance for Research on Schizophrenia and Depression; Black Mental Health Alliance; Anxiety Disorders Association of America; AIM-Awareness; ACT-MAD; MadNation; The Support Coalition; Shocked; Families, USA; Public Citizen Health Research Group; and Psychiatric Survivors Advocacy/Liberation Movement. The following resources can be used to find these and other advocacy groups:

The National Mental Health Services Knowledge Exchange Network (KEN). KEN provides information about mental health through toll-free telephone services, an electronic bulletin board, and publications. KEN was developed for users of mental health services and their families, the general public, policy makers, service providers, and the media. KEN is a national one-stop source of information and resources on prevention, treatment, and rehabilitation services for mental illness.

KEN can be contacted at: KEN, P.O. Box 42490, Washington, DC 20015, Phone: 800.769.CMHS (weekdays from 8:30 a.m. to 5 p.m. EST), Fax: 301.984.8796, TDD: 301.443.9006, Web: www.mentalhealth.org.

National Institute of Mental Health (NIMH). NIMH advocacy work is done through educating the public on various mental and brain disorders through publications and nationwide prevention education programs. NIMH offers the public a number of informative materials on mental health topics. The Institute also offers toll-free information lines for specific disorders.

NIMH can be contacted at: NIMH, 5600 Fishers Lane, Room 7C-02, MSC 8030, Bethesda, MD 20892-8030, Phone:

301.443.4536, Web: www.nimh.nih.gov.

Self Help Clearinghouse. A resource for national and local self-help groups. The clearinghouse publishes a guide to self-help groups and operates a toll-free referral number: 800.FOR.MASH.

National Mental Health Consumer's Self-Help Clearinghouse. Another resource offering a toll-free information and referral line: 800.553.4539. This resource can also be accessed by writing: 1211 Chestnut Street, Suite 1000, Philadelphia, PA 19107.

Internet. Browse the web for the web sites of particular advocacy groups or those offering links to mental health web sites. The following web sites may be particularly helpful:

- www.mhsource.com
- www.handsnet.org (NAPAS)
- www.qeeg.npi.ucla.edu/advocacy
- www.klinks.com/generalinfo
- www.radix.net/ccd (Consortium for Citizens with Disabilities)
- member.aol.com/jimhofw/links.htm (Mental Health Web Sites)
- www.compeer.org
- www.protectionandadvocacy.com/odis.htm (Links to disability-related organizations)
- www.naotd.org/advocacy.htm (Links to advocacy web sites)

Furthermore, using the following key words will help counselors to find additional information on advocacy groups on the Internet: "mental health advocacy," "protection and advocacy," "support and advocacy," and, by typing in a particular topic, such as "depression."

Additional Resources

Encyclopedia of Associations. A reference guide to approximately 23,000 national and international organizations. Maurer, Christine & Sheets, Tara E. (1982). Encyclopedia of associations: An association unlimited reference. New York: Gale.

National Directory of Mental Health Advocacy Programs. Lists over 400 mental health rights protection and advocacy programs, including legal organizations, ex-patient groups, parents and family groups, mental health associations, and patients' rights programs operating within departments of mental health. Greenberg, P., Freddolino, P. & Lecklitener, G. (1982). National directory of mental health advocacy programs. Los Angeles: Human Interaction Research Institute.

Megan K. Tenety is a Family Preservation Services Therapist at Catholic Charities of Hunterdon County, N.J. Mark S. Kiselica is an associate professor and co-chairperson in the department of counseling and personnel services at The College of New Jersey in Ewing, N.J.

Chapter Fifteen

Advocacy and Indigenous Methods of Healing

Derald Wing Sue

As a counselor, how would you work with culturally different clients who believe that (a) their personal problems were due to spirit possession, (b) only a shaman with special powers could understand the disorder, (c) answers could only be obtained by a journey into the spirit world, and (d) cures could only be accomplished through a formal ritual (chanting, incense burning, symbolic sacrifice, etc.)? Some of you might assume that these clients suffer from delusions, lack contact with reality, or you might try to convince them that spirits do not exist.

Most of us who have had very little experience with indigenous methods of healing would find great difficulty in working effectively with such clients. Yet, the increasing numbers of racial/ethnic minority groups in our society, especially recent Asian, Latin American, and African immigrants, have exposed helping professionals to a host of different belief systems, some radically different from our own, but many with familiar parallels. As counselors working with client groups who differ from them in race, culture, and ethnicity, it seems important to study and understand indigenous healing practices and our potential role as advocates.

Indigenous healing can be defined as helping beliefs and practices that originate over extended time within the culture, that are not transported from other regions, and that are designed for treating the inhabitants of the given group. Those who study indigenous psychologies do not make an a priori assumption that one particular perspective is superior to another. Most non-Western indigenous healing beliefs share certain assumptions:

(a) problems reside in relationships with people and spirits;

(b) harmony and balance in the family and nature are

desirable;

c) healing must involve the entire group and not just an individual;

(d) spirituality, prayer, and ritual are important aspects of healing;

(e) the helper is a respected elder of the family or community; and

(f) the method of healing is culture specific.

Rationale

Even the American Psychiatric Association in the *Diagnostic and Statistical Manual-IV* (*DSM-IV*) acknowledges the importance of ethnic and cultural factors related to psychiatric diagnosis. They warn that clinicians who work with immigrant and ethnic minorities must take into account: (a) the predominant means of manifesting disorders (e.g., possessing spirits, nerves, fatalism, and inexplicable misfortune), (b) culture-specific explanatory models, and (c) preferences for indigenous sources of care. Let me use a real life case example (Tobin & Friedman, 1983) to illustrate these points.

Spirit attacks and shamanic cure: The case of Vang Xiong

In 1980, a former Laotian Hmong soldier, Vang Xiong, resettled in Chicago with his wife and child. In addition to the trauma associated with his escape from Laos, and witnessing the horrendous torture and death of his comrades and relatives, the adjustment to unfamiliar surroundings in an urban area caused extreme culture shock. Several months after his arrival, Vang's problems began.

Vang had difficulty sleeping and frequently had disturbing dreams. His fitful sleep was dominated by dreams of a cat or dog sitting on his chest making it extremely difficult to breath. The most frightening nightmare, however, was when a tall female spirit came to his bed and lay on top of him. He could not breath and was near suffocation when he would awaken screaming. Vang strongly believed that his death was imminent. After many sleepless nights, Vang came to see his resettlement worker, a young bilingual Hmong man named Moua Lee. Lee was aware of the many inexplicable deaths which occurred among the recent refugees—known as the "Hmong Sudden Death Syndrome." It generally occurred within the first two years of residence in the United States. Autopsies produced no identifiable cause for the deaths. All the reports were the same—a person in apparently good health went to sleep and died without awakening. Often, the victim displayed labored breathing, screams, and frantic movements just before death. With this dire possibility for Vang, the mental health staff felt they lacked the expertise for so complex and potentially dangerous a case. Conventional western means of treatment for other similarly afflicted Hmong clients had proven minimally effective.

Fortunately, Lee successfully served as an advocate on behalf of his client. He cited countless examples of such cases which were successfully treated in his homeland; convinced the staff that Vang's belief in the spirit world had similarities to the world of the unconscious; sought out consultation with Hmong elders in the community; argued against policies preventing the use of nontraditional healing methods; and enlisted the aid of a highly respected shaman, Mrs. Thor. While the social services agency remained skeptical, they finally saw no other option and finally consented to Lee's request. The description of the treatment is given below:

> That evening, Mrs. Thor arrived at the home of Vang Xiong and listened to his story, asked a few questions, and then told him she thought she could help. She gathered the Xiong family around the dining room table, upon which she placed some candles alongside many plates of food that Vang's wife had prepared. Mrs. Thor lit the candles, and then began a chant that Vang and his wife knew was an attempt to communicate with spirits. ... Approximately one hour after she had begun, Mrs. Thor completed her chanting, announcing that she knew what was wrong...she had learned from her spirit that the figures in Vang's dreams who lay on his chest and who made it so difficult for him to breathe were the souls of the apartment's previous tenants, who had apparently moved out so abruptly they had left their souls behind. Mrs. Thor constructed a cloak out of newspaper for Vang to wear. She then cut the cloak in two, and burned the pieces, sending the spirits on their way with the smoke. She also had Vang crawl through a hoop, and then between two knives, telling him that these maneuvers would make it very hard for spirits to follow. Following these brief ceremonies, the food prepared by Vang's wife was enjoyed by all. The leftover

meats were given in payment to Mrs. Thor, and she left, assuring Vang Xiong that his troubles with spirits were over. (p. 441)

Since undergoing the healing ceremony in which the unhappy spirits were released, Vang has reported no more problems with nightmares or with his breathing during sleep.

Such a story might appear unbelievable and akin to mysticism to readers. Most of us have been trained in a Western ontology which does not embrace indigenous nor alternative healing approaches. Indeed, if anything, it actively rejects such approaches as unscientific and supernatural; counselors are encouraged to rely on sensory information, defined by the physical plane of existence rather than the spiritual one. Such a rigid stance is unfortunate and short-sighted because there is much that counselors can learn from these age-old forms of treatment. Unfortunately, space does not allow for a discussion of the evidence supporting indigenous healing.

The Role of an Advocate

Were it not for Lee who acted as an advocate on behalf of Vang, he might not be alive today. Because counselors are increasingly being asked to work with culturally different clients, and because they now realize that the conventional one-to-one, in-the-office, talk-form of treatment may be at odds with the cultural views of their clients, they are finding their traditional therapeutic role ineffective. Advocacy roles share certain commonalties (D.W. Sue, et.al, 1998):

(a) They are generally characterized by the more active helping style of the counselor;

(b) They often involve the counselor working outside the office and in the home, institution, or community of the client;

(c) The role of the counselor is more externally focused and directed toward changing environmental conditions such as policies and practices of an organization, enhancing job opportunities, etc. as opposed to focusing on and changing the client;

(d) Clients are not perceived as having a problem (internal pathology), but as experiencing one (problematic situations);

(e) The advocacy role emphasizes prevention as well as

remediation; and

(f) The counselor shoulders an increased responsibility for determining the course and outcome of the helping process.

The advocate role entails representing the person's or group's best interests to other individuals, groups, or organizations. Advocates may, for example, represent a person who does not speak English well and argue on their behalf for fair and equitable treatment. The role is not a neutral one and may entail sociopolitical dimensions.

Becoming an Advocate for Indigenous Healing

More than anything else, indigenous healing and advocacy are community oriented and focused. Culturally competent counselors must begin to expand their definition of the helping role to encompass greater community involvement. The conventional counselor role, oftentimes, is nonfunctional in minority communities. Becoming an effective advocate for indigenous healing requires increased sensitivity and knowledge acquisition. Reading books about non-western belief systems and attending seminars and lectures on the topic are valuable and helpful, but understanding culturally different perspectives must be supplemented by "lived experience." Because the United States has become so diverse, one need not leave the country to experience the richness of different cultures and belief systems. Opportunities abound. I suggest that counselors consider attending cultural events, meetings, and activities of culturally different groups in the community. Such actions allow you to view minority individuals interacting in their community and how their values are expressed in relationships. Hearing from church leaders, attending open community forums, and attending community celebrations allow you to sense the strengths of the minority community, observe leadership in action, personalizes your understanding; and it allows you to identify potential guides and advisors to your own self-enlightenment.

Mental health professionals must be willing and able to form partnerships with indigenous healers or develop community liaisons if they are to become effective advocates. Such an outreach has several advantages:

(a) traditional healers may provide knowledge and insights into client populations which would prove of value to the delivery of counseling services,

(b) such an alliance will ultimately enhance the cultural credibility of counselors, and

(c) it allows for referral to traditional healers (shamans, religious leaders, etc.) in which treatment is rooted in cultural traditions. To accomplish these goals, counselors must respect the universal shamanic tradition while still being embedded in a Western psychological tradition. Most culturally different clients are open to a blend of both western and non-western approaches.

References

Sue, D.W., Carter, R.T., Casas, J.M., Fouad N.A., Ivey, A.E., Jensen, M., LaFromboise, T., Manese, J.E., Ponterotto, J.G., & Vazquez-Nutall, E. (1998). *Multicultural Counseling Competencies: Individual and Organizational Development*. Thousand Oaks, CA: Sage.

Sue, D.W. & Sue, D. (1999).*Counseling The Culturally Different: Theory and Practice*. Third Edition. New York: John Wiley and Sons.

Tobin, J.J., & Friedman, J. (1983). Spirits, shamans, and nightmare death: Survivor stress in a Hmong refugee. *American Journal of Orthopsychiatry, 53*, 439-448.

Derald Wing Sue is a professor at the California School of Professional Psychology, Alameda, and at the California State University, Hayward.

Chapter Sixteen

Advocating for Women in the Criminal Justice and Addiction Treatment Systems

Karen Kelly & Gwen Empson

During the past 150 years, women have made up a far greater portion of drug users than has usually been recognized. Despite this fact, treatment issues for drug-abusing women have received very little attention. Increasing numbers of women dealing with drug-related issues find themselves treated not in community settings but in the criminal justice system. Currently, women represent 30 percent of the drug-abusing population but are entering the prison system at a rate two times that of men (NIDA, 1998). How can we as practitioners meet the pressing needs of offender women in treatment, prisons, and jails through the 1990s and the millennium? The correctional environment poses special advocacy challenges.

Advocacy Issues for Women in the Criminal Justice System

The role of advocate can no longer be performed by any one single entity. As advocates for quality service delivery, counselors and providers of care must collaborate with clients and others advocating for changes in public policy. Advocacy involves clients, their families, and the community.

In today's cost-driven treatment systems, women who are regarded as criminals seek treatment but face a number of barriers to essential elements of quality care. These barriers may include limited access to outpatient treatment, acceptance into jail without evaluation for drug abuse, or unavailability of prison-based programs.

There are nearly six times as many women incarcerated in prison today as there were in 1930—the numbers rose by 460 percent, from 12,331 to 69,028. More than three times as many women are incarcerated today as there were in 1983. From 1983 to 1994, the number of incarcerated women grew by 212 percent, from 15,652 to 48,900. This flood into prisons has been correlated with the increasingly punitive legal response to drug-related behavior, the lack of viable treatment, and few alternative community sanctions for women (Owen & Bloom, 1995).

Correctional institutions vary in type and quality of services provided to treat women when addressing their substance abuse, addiction, family, health, and related social problems. Most of these women are single parents. They may lack extended family and may already be in the social welfare system. In addition, many women with substance abuse problems are victims of physical abuse, domestic violence, and rape. Many have experienced sexual abuse and incest as children. The psychological impact of violence includes mood disorders, including depression, posttraumatic stress disorder, and low self-esteem. Addicted women offenders usually feel powerless and victimized, with personal boundaries so violated that they lack a clear vision of self (CSAT, 1996). Even in community health settings, let alone correctional institutions, treatment based on traditional models rarely addresses these issues to the degree that is needed.

Advocacy as Empowerment

The overall environment in a prison or jail can be supportive for treatment or it can be non-responsive, setting up a series of structural, physical, and emotional barriers for the staff and clients of treatment programs. Institutional support is important from two levels, from administrators and from the overall institution, especially security staff. As advocates, counselors and service providers can help to ensure that women offenders are receiving the services needed to meet their unique situations. With many of the prison-based programs currently eliminating educational services, women who do not have high school or general equivalency diplomas, job training, or usable employment skills find themselves with little or no support when they are released to return to their families and communities.

Many times, improving a client's life may require direct advocacy activities such as writing a letter to a judge, the warden, or a family member to assist the client's reentry into society after treatment and/or incarceration. Advocacy also includes empowering clients and improving their environment. Many counselors and service providers, limited by time and other constraints, must find time to fully inform their clients about programs, services, policies, and expectations. Client advocacy requires that clients be guided through a maze of difficult choices and changes.

Substance abuse treatment programs, jails, and prisons are usually not productive grounds for working with women who need to come to terms with their traumatic histories of abuse and lack of power. These programs are often rigid and authoritarian, making it difficult for women to reconnect to other people and discover their capacities for trust, autonomy, initiative, competence, identity, and intimacy. Treatment programs, counselors, and service providers are likely to face obstacles when advocating for the development of healthy environments in which counseling and treatment can address alcohol and drug-related issues, social problems, and lifestyle changes. Providing services for offender women in correctional treatment settings requires a coming together of two systems where the goals and philosophy are different: the incarceration environment where the concerns are punitive and the community setting where the goals are supportive and rehabilitative. In contrast to the criminal justice system, the treatment system is expected to place its highest priority on the well-being of the individual person rather than focusing on the crime committed and its consequences for society. The primary concern and responsibility of the treatment system is a healthier individual.

Critical Issues in Advocating for Change

Part of advocacy is informing clients that they have a right to high-quality treatment. However, these services must be available. Currently, services to address the needs of offender women are not always available or accessible. The following critical issues require our undivided attention and advocacy regarding public policy:

- Providing opportunities for family reunification. Involving children and significant others is possible in jail and prison settings and is a promising strategy for helping incarcerated women.
- Providing health care. Full medical services are needed for offender women with substance abuse problems. Many of these women arrive in prison after long periods of physical or sexual abuse, homelessness, and neglected health needs.

- Preventive counseling for HIV and sexually-transmitted diseases.
- Programming for coexisting psychiatric disorders, including depression.
- Identifying issues related to medicating. For example, some women may be overmedicating to block emotional pain.
- Special programming for pregnant women, focusing on their special needs in terms of medical care and treatment protocols.
- Programming for education and vocational training.
- Training for staff including security officers.
- Hiring and training appropriate personnel for treatment programs.
- Determining appropriate racial, ethnic, and gender mix.
- Recruiting staff from the treatment environment and program graduates.

Finding Solutions

Our job as advocates for treatment services to women offenders is to inform the public and our legislators about the problems related to addiction treatment for incarcerated women and about appropriate solutions. We have to trust that public opinion will be supportive of addressing these needs and that people, when informed, will influence policy makers to do what is right.

A collaborative effort among criminal justice personnel, jails, prison-based treatment programs, and community organizations can provide the healthy environments that women offenders need. We need to be of help to our clients by listening carefully to them and by monitoring the services that affect their lives.

Providers of these specialized services must look to other organizations and agencies both to find common agreement and to provide support. The use of research that clearly documents what works will aid counselors and providers of treatment and advocacy immeasurably when it comes time to present legislative initiatives. Empowering clients to become their own advocates by supporting meetings and rallies that ask for client testimony and experiences is also critical to forming public opinion.

As service delivery changes and treatment for substance abuse becomes less available, both providers and recipients of treatment feel the impact. Roadblocks such as unfair laws, cost containment, and unavailability of treatment can and will impact the services provided to offender women. As providers of substance abuse treatment services in communities, jails, and prisons, all of us should be client advocates first and foremost.

References

Owen, B., & Bloom, B. (1995). Profiling women prisoners: Findings from national surveys and a California sample. *The Prison Journal, 75 (2)*, 165-185.

Center for Substance Abuse Treatment (CSAT). (1994). *Practical approaches in the treatment of women who abuse alcohol and other drugs.* Rockville, MD: Department of Health and Human Services, Public Health Service.

National Institution on Drug Abuse (NIDA). (1998). *Drug addiction research and the health of women. Executive summary.* Rockville, MD: Department of Health and Human Services, Public Health Service.

Karen Kelly is the director of the Addiction Technology Transfer Center at the Morehouse School of Medicine in Atlanta. Gwen Empson is the director of Correctional Medical Services in New Castle, Del.

ERIC
Resources

Supplementary ERIC
Resources

This section contains over two dozen individual resources gleaned from an ERIC/CASS search on advocacy. For the most part, they are either ERIC Digests, abstracts of longer ERIC documents, or brief annotations regarding journal articles relevant to advocacy as presented in this publication. They are illustrative of the rich vein of resources on advocacy available through ERIC. Many of the resources listed contain extensive bibliographies of additional resources.

At the end of this section is information on how you can obtain the resources listed. It also identifies how you can undertake your own ERIC search to obtain additional resources. If you wish more information on ERIC searches, please contact ERIC/CASS at 800-414-9769 or E-mail us at ericcass@uncg.edu.

Record 1 of 25 - ERIC

AN: ED425249

AU: Schwartz,-Wendy

TI: The Schooling of Multiracial Students. ERIC/CUE Digest, Number138.

CS: ERIC Clearinghouse on Urban Education, New York, NY.

PY: 1998

ISSN: 0889-8049

AV: ERIC Clearinghouse on Urban Education, Institute for Urban and Minority Education, Teachers College, Box 40, Columbia University, New York, NY 10027 (free).

DE: *Child-Development; *Elementary-Secondary-Education; *Equal-Education; *Racial-Identification; *Teaching-Methods

DE:Curriculum-Development; Models-; Multicultural-Education; Professional-Development; Racial-Differences; Self-Concept; Teacher-Attitudes; Teacher-Role; Urban-Youth

ID: *Mixed-Race-Persons; *Multiracial-Education

ID: ERIC-Digests; Identity-Formation

AB: The purpose of this digest is to help educators develop a curriculum for multiracial students that fosters their ability to develop a positive identity and achieve academically. To this end, the digest briefly reviews identity formation in multiracial children and then presents schoolwide and classroom strategies that have been shown to be particularly effective with multiracial students and that also promote all children's understanding of racial issues. Multiracial identity development is a complex process that is only now being defined, as researchers have determined that models of minority identity development are not appropriate for multiracial individuals and that models based on deficits in development seriously shortchange multiracial individuals. A model recently developed by W. Poston (1990) provides a typology of stages through which some families progress as they help their children define themselves personally and develop connections to their heritages. It is important for schools to foster universal respect for students. The message that educators convey about how they view multicultural families is important to the developing self-concept of children, but how best to serve these students educationally is an area of professional development still being defined. Educators should consider their own views about multiracial students, and they should elicit information from multiracial families so that they can communicate more effectively and sensitively with their students. Teachers can facilitate age-appropriate discussions about racial issues and can plan curricula and activities to support the identity formation of their multiracial students. School counselors can also use sensitive approaches to help educators by affirming the right of all students to be treated on an individual basis. Educators can foster the best in all students by helping them appreciate the uniqueness of each individual. (Contains 16 references.) (SLD)

TX: The number of multiracial children in the U.S. is increasing: more than 100,000 have been born annually over the last decade, and most interracial families reside in urban areas (Okun, 1996; U.S. Bureau of the Census, cited in Root, 1996). Therefore, it is necessary for educators and counselors to understand and meet the special needs of students of mixed heritage and to support their families' efforts to nurture them. Children of mixed racial and ethnic heritage have unique advantages. They also experience particular challenges. Individuals who are socialized as multiracial frequently have an enhanced sense of self and identity, and greater intergroup tolerance, language facility, appreciation of minority group cultures, and ties to single-heritage groups than do monoracial people (Thornton, 1996). On the other hand, developing a positive identity may be more difficult for multiracial children than for others, the result of a combination of personal feelings about their identity choices, the way they are socialized within their family, and the attitudes and pressures they encounter when they begin to function in society (Morrissey, 1996). Further, the racism visited upon people of color generally in the U.S. may be exacerbated by a corollary, and possibly even stronger, prejudice of some people against mixing races through marriage and procreation (Miller & Rotheram-Borus, 1994; Pinderhughes, 1995) and "blurring the physical categories upon which white status and power depend" (Wilson, 1987, p. 7). While black-white marriages comprise the lowest rate of intermarriage, the families they create elicit the strongest negative reactions (Okun, 1996), possibly because they are more noticeable than other interracial families or because racism against African Americans has historically been stronger than racism against other groups.

THE MULTIRACIAL POPULATION Ethnic group differences have a significant impact on children's social development, although the impact varies with age and specific ethnicity. How multiracial children are labeled by themselves, their families, and society in general is an important factor in their lives, for labels are powerful comments on how an individual's existence is viewed. The term "multiracial" is now favored to designate an individual's mixed heritage. It covers people not only of mixed race, but monoracial people of mixed ethnicity, language, and culture. Further, monoracial children who were adopted by parents of a different race often consider themselves multiracial as their lives incorporate the cultures of both their biological and adoptive parents. "Multiracial" is used here to indicate individuals of mixed racial, ethnic, or cultural ancestry whose lives reflect multiple heritages.

STAGES OF IDENTITY DEVELOPMENT Multiracial identity development is a complex process that is only now being defined as researchers have determined that models of minority identity development are not appropriate for multiracial individuals and that models based on deficits in development seriously shortchange multiracial individuals. One recently-created model of racial identity development meshes existing research on personal identity (which includes constructs such as self-esteem, self-worth, and interpersonal competence) and reference group orientation (constructs such as racial identity, racial esteem, and racial ideology) to define stages of development reflecting the impact of heritage. The stages range from an individual's initial acquisition of a personal identity (which does not encompass racial factors) to satisfaction with his or her ultimate decision about group identification after working through various conflicts related to the need to make such a choice. The model's last stage is integration of all the components of an individual's heritage (Poston, 1990). This model provides a typology of the stages that some families progress through as they help their children define themselves personally and develop connections to their heritages. However, the model does not fit the children of multiracial families choosing to embrace only one culture.

ATTITUDES TOWARDS CLASSIFICATION Within the multiracial community there are several alternative views on classification. Some people want to be classified solely as human, asserting that any designation other than "white" relegates them to a lower status, given existing racism (Pinderhughes, 1995). Other families, perhaps the majority, help their children develop a multiracial identity that promotes equal pride in all the components of their heritage (Pinderhughes, 1995). Still others—single parents, especially, who opt to emphasize their own race—foster a monoracial identity for their children. Some do so because the children most closely resemble members of a certain race; others do so because they are knowledgeable about only one of their children's heritages (Mills, 1994). In particular, some parents of children with African ancestry raise them as black in order to prepare them for their treatment (including victimization by racism) as such (Morrison & Rodgers, 1996).

SCHOOL PRACTICES Multiracial children need to be exposed to models of all the ethnicities they comprise and to multiracial models. They also need to live and learn in a supportive community that affirms multiracialism, to understand what it means to be multiracial, and to acquire culturally-linked coping skills. The existence of multiracial children challenges prevailing assumptions about natural divisions between people, and assignment of traits based on race. Optimally, in school, these children "will serve as creative resources for developing new forms of polyglot cultural creativity" (Chiong, 1998, p. 109). This is not to say that they should be treated as one more race to be identified, assigned specific personal traits and learning expectations, and segregated. Rather, multicultural children, with their particular contributions to discourse in the classroom, should encourage educators to consider the needs and strengths of individuals rather than groups, and to reject all race-based stereotypes (Glass & Wallace, 1996). It is important for schools to foster universal respect for students, to be clear that intolerance by either staff or students is not acceptable, and to provide their staffs with accurate information on multiculturalism so they can correct misconceptions when they hear them from other adults or children (Morrison & Rodgers, 1996). School people need to be vigilant to ensure that no children are victimized by others, however subtly, and that the identity chosen by students is accepted and respected by their peers.

THE ROLE OF EDUCATORS The message that educators convey about how they view multicultural families is important to the developing self-concept of children, but how best to serve multiracial students educationally is an area of professional development still being defined. As the trend toward distinguishing between members of different ethnic groups and between members of the same ethnic group continues, in recognition of the fact that "lumping" is neither appropriate nor useful, interest in better meeting the specific needs of multiracial students is increasing. The traditional "deficit model" for these students, which led educators to assume that they were rife with problems in need of solving, is slowly giving way to the belief that the needs of multiracial students are neither different from those of other students, nor more severe. Further, since multiracial children may identify themselves in many different ways, it is important for educators to reflect and respect the preferences of individual children when alluding to their heritage.

CONSIDERING PERSONAL VIEWS ON RACE AND MULTIRACIALISM In order to develop empathy for multiracial children in general, educators should understand how people from other cultures view their world; to do so for a specific multiracial child, they should learn how that child views the world. Further, educators need to examine their personal values with regard to interracial marriage and families, and consider whether society's historical court-supported disapproval of race mixing has influenced them. They should ask themselves if they automatically categorize a multiracial child as a member of a generic or specific minority group, and if doing so shortchanges the student in terms of respect and expectations. Educators need to identify the unique characteristics of each child, instead of assuming that all children who share a heritage share the same complement of characteristics. Learning about different ethnicities will help educators understand that there are vast differences within groups, including physical, religious, economic, political, and educational. There are also differences in the appearance of members of the same ethnic group as well as similarities in appearance across groups, so it is not useful to assume a child's ethnicity can be determined by physical characteristics. It is important, too, for educators to recognize that cultural factors, in both historical and current contexts, influence children's development and can serve to explain certain attitudes and behavior (Wardle, 1989).

ELICITING INFORMATION FROM MULTIRACIAL FAMILIES. It is important for educators to know about the heritage, in all of its possible complexity, of their students. Such information can further help teachers transcend any negative attitudes about multiracialism they may have absorbed from living in a largely race-based society (Glass & Wallace, 1996). Parent-teacher conferences, preferably held at the start of a child's schooling, can be a forum for learning about students' backgrounds. To alleviate any discomfort with questions about ethnic background, educators can employ a questionnaire created by the anti-bias task force of the National Association for the Education of Young Children which facilitates supportive querying (cited in Morrison & Rodgers, 1996). This information helps educators more effectively and sensitively communicate with their students. It will also enable them to encourage multiracial children to show pride in all their ethnicities. In addition, teachers should know in advance that some children, when doing a project on their heritage, will quite correctly present material on several cultures.

MEETING THE DEVELOPMENTAL NEEDS OF MULTIRACIAL STUDENTS. How well multiracial children form a cohesive identity within a society that favors racial purity is largely determined by family and community support which enables them to reflect and take pride in all their heritages (Chiong, 1998). Thus, it is important for educators to support and accept them; to help children develop the skills and confidence to protect themselves from verbal and physical abuse; and to explore with the children who abuse, the reasons why they do so, and to make it clear that such behavior cannot be tolerated in school (Wardle, 1987, 1992). They can also help students feel a sense of community, especially important if their parents' interracial marriage, or their own interracial adoption, has caused rifts in their extended family (Miller & Rotheram-Borus, 1994).

SCHOOL ACTIVITIES AND CURRICULUM All aspects of school life can support multiracial children and counter racism that children of all ethnicities see in society at large. In general, teachers can facilitate age-appropriate discussions and foster open and supportive questioning about race. It is natural for young children to ask questions like "Are you black?" and teachers need to be ready to help children respond in a way that builds their self-concept and educates the questioner (Morrison & Rodgers, 1996; Wardle, 1992). One educational and engaging project, which can be schoolwide or involve only a single class, is developing and sharing family trees. Students can go back as far as possible to develop their own tree, questioning their families, and seeking out illustrative artifacts. Teachers can help adopted students research aspects of their heritage not shared by their current family. Parents or other relatives can be invited to talk to the class or participate in a group activity (Wardle, 1987). In addition, schools can do the following (Morrison & Rodgers, 1996; Wardle, 1987, 1992):

- •Celebrate many heritages, stressing their interplay in life and the ways that different cultures have similar commemorations.

- •Provide toys for younger children which include dolls with multiracial characteristics.

- •Include multiracial persons as role models when selecting assembly speakers and other resource persons.

- •Seek out and use the increasing number of children's books available that depict multiracialism in the classroom, acquire them for the school library, and request that the local library purchase them for family use.

167

Curriculum can include study units on art, music, and literature, which transcend ethnic boundaries, instead of units on specific groups, such as "Indians" (Wardle, 1987). Curriculum can diminish differences between cultures by refraining from breaking groups into specific categories defined by color and physical attributes. Specifically, at the appropriate grade level, curriculum can do the following (Morrison & Rodgers, 1996; Wardle, 1996):

- Present information on, and show pictures of, people of many racial and ethnic groups, including those of mixed heritage.

- Demonstrate how people in the U.S. have successfully mixed languages, cultures, and religions throughout its history, and how the country has always been a home to multiethnic people (for example, early settlers whose parents comprised different European heritages).

- Identify multiracial heroes such as Frederick Douglass and James Audubon, and cultural figures like Maria Tallchief and Paula Abdul.

- Cover the current status of multiracial people around the world, such as Mestizos, Creoles, and Brazilians.

- Address directly the history of racism against groups of people, including the multiracial population, and discuss the reasons for it.

- Study monoracial groups to promote an understanding of the role of race in society by exploring why some people need to belong to an exclusive group or need to feel superior to others, and what the societal and personal consequences of such attitudes are.

COUNSELING School counselors need to provide an accurate assessment and intervention for students of color, and to understand how historical and current racism impacts the lives of individuals of all ethnicities (Okun, 1996). With regard to multiracial children, counselors should help them develop a positive racial identity, possibly in the face of challenges imposed by monoracial groups that resist acceptance of blending (Morrissey, 1996). To provide services most usefully, counselors must reconsider race-based preconceptions resulting from erroneous assumptions. Traditionally, for example, it has been thought that multiracial children have problems, identity conflicts in particular, because they "must choose" a race (Wilson, 1987, p. 7). It has also been believed that the problems they do have, which seem to have no bearing on their racial composition, are nevertheless race-related. Both these beliefs can result in overlooking the real causes of a student's problems and, thus, can sharply limit the benefits of the counseling. Conversely, exploration of clients' attitudes about their identity and heritage can reveal that a problem (such as depression or family difficulties), which on the surface is not race-related, actually is (Adler, 1987). Multiracial teenage clients may need special supports. While all adolescents experience conflicts in identity development, those of multiracial youth may be exacerbated by a desire to find a dating partner who matches, or simply respects, their heritage; or by their peer groups' newly-manifested ostracism, resulting from a heightened emphasis on conformity. To best work with young multiracial clients, counselors should do the following (Adler, 1987; Poston, 1990; Morrissey, 1996; Okun, 1996):

- Understand the racial identity development process.

- Develop counseling processes and goals that are consistent with the individual differences and cultural orientations of their clients.

- Create a culturally sensitive counseling climate, and demonstrate respect and compassion for clients and validation of their multiple heritages.

- Learn about each client's heritage, and when appropriate, participate in local ethnic events, alone or with clients.

- Learn about the cultural and experiential differences of each client within a sociopolitical context.

- Help clients explore issues related to differences between the counselor's and client's heritage, and help clients feel confident that those differences will not compromise the effectiveness of the counseling process.

- Encourage clients to discuss personal feelings about identity and ethnic affiliation, since many families do not emphasize issues of heritage, despite recent increased public attention to multiracial pride. Create a safe atmosphere where clients can express feelings of alienation and anger.

- Help clients understand that they may have internalized the biased attitudes of others about their heritage, and help them move from an external to an internal perspective of self.

- Consider the effects on clients of family and personal stresses related to race-related conflicts and racism.

- Offer to work with families to help them fully accept their multiracial children, enable them to foster their children's positive racial identity development, and promote their children's interest in exploring all their heritages.

- Learn about available community resources and support groups for clients and their families.

References

Adler, A.J. (1987). Children and biracial identity. In J. Grimes & A. Thomas (Eds.), Children's needs: Psychological perspectives (pp. 56-60). (ED 353 487)

Chiong, J.A. (1998). Racial categorization of multiracial children in schools. Bergin & Garvey: Westport, CT.

Glass, R.D., & Wallace, K.R. (1996). Challenging race and racism. In M.P.Root (Ed.), The multicultural experience: Racial borders as the new frontier (pp. 341-358). Thousand Oaks, CA: Sage. (ED 393 956)

Miller, R.L., & Rotheram-Borus. (1994). Growing up biracial in the United States. In E.P. Salett & D.R. Koslow (Eds.), Race ethnicity and self (pp. 143-169). Washington, DC: National Multicultural Institute. (ED 374 190)

Mills, C. (1994, Summer). Doing the right thing. Biracial child, 1(3), 10.

Morrison, J.W., & Rodgers, L.S. (1996, November). Being responsive to the needs of children from dual heritage backgrounds. Young Children, 52(1), 29-33. (EJ 533 092)

Morrissey, M. (1996, November). Rising number of interracial children presenting new challenges for counselors. Counseling Today, 1, 8, 24–25.

Okun, B.F. (1996). Understanding diverse families: What practitioners need to know. New York: Guilford. (ED 410 001)

Pinderhughes, E. (1995). Biracial identity—Asset or handicap? In H.W. Harris, H.C. Blue, & E.E.H. Griffith (Eds.), Racial and ethnic identity: Psychological development and creative expression (pp. 73-93). New York: Routledge. (ED 389 762).

Poston, W.S.C. (1990, November-December). The biracial identity development model: A needed addition. Journal of Counseling and Development, 69(2), 152-55. (EJ 424 084).

Root, M.P.P. (1996). A significant frontier. In M.P.P. Root (Ed.), The multicultural experience: Racial borders as the new frontier (pp. xiii-xxviii). Thousand Oaks, CA: Sage. (ED 393 956)

Thornton, M.C. (1996). Hidden agendas, identity theories, and multiracial people. In M.P.P. Root (Ed.), The multicultural experience: Racial borders as the new frontier (pp. 101-120). Thousand Oaks, CA: Sage. (ED 393 956)

Wardle, F. (1987, January). Are you sensitive to interracial children's special needs? Young Children, 42(2), pp. 53-59. (EJ 347 857)

Wardle, F. (1989, July-August). Children of mixed parentage: How can professionals respond? Children Today, 18(4), pp. 10-13. (EJ 394 112)

Wardle, F. (1992, May). Supporting biracial children in the school setting. Education and Treatment of Children, 15(2), 163-72. (EJ 454 421)

Wilson, A. (1987). Mixed race children: A study of identity. London: Allen & Unwin.

This Digest was developed by the ERIC Clearinghouse on Urban Education with funding from the Office of Educational Research and Improvement, U.S. Department of Education, under contract no. RR93002016. The opinions in this Digest do not necessarily reflect the position or policies of OERI or the Department of Education.

Record 2 of 25 - ERIC

AN: ED419033

TI:Making Colleges and Universities Safe for Gay and Lesbian Students. Report and Recommendations of the Governor's Commission on Gay and Lesbian Youth.

CS:Massachusetts Governor's Commission on Gay and Lesbian Youth, Boston.

PY:1993

DE:*College-Students; *Homophobia-; *Homosexuality-; *School-Safety; *Social-Discrimination

DE:Curriculum-Development; Educational-Policy; Higher-Education; Minority-Groups; Training-

ID: *Massachusetts-

AB: In the 1992-93 academic year, the Higher Education Committee of the Massachusetts Governor's Commission on Gay and Lesbian Youth heard testimony and conducted focus groups with a cross section of students, faculty, and administrators from a number of colleges and universities in Massachusetts. This report is the result of these meetings. The Commission learned that even in colleges and universities that already have clearly stated antidiscrimination statutes that include sexual orientation, sexual minorities still often feel excluded. Additional education and advocacy are needed to ensure that sexual minorities are not subjected to insensitivity, harassment, and violence. An introduction discusses the history of efforts by gay and lesbians for equal standing in institutions of higher education and identifies problems that they face, from discrimination, harassment and violence to suicide.

Recommendations for more equity for gay, lesbian, and trans-sexual students are made in the areas of: (1) educational policies; (2) training and development; (3) services; (4) curriculum, educational materials, and academic affairs; (5) employee concerns; and (6) community and off-campus concerns. Five appendixes contain information on student organizational development, samples of college policies, local and national journals and publications, lists of local and national resources, and a list of electronic networking resources. (Contains 24 references and the executive order establishing the commission.) (SLD)

Record 3 of 25 - ERIC

AN: ED417372

AU: Lee,-Courtland-C., ed.; Walz,-Garry-R., ed.

TI: Social Action: A Mandate for Counselors.

CS: American Counseling Association, Alexandria, VA.; ERIC Clearinghouse on Counseling and Student Services, Greensboro, NC.

PY: 1998

ISBN:155620213X

AV: American Counseling Association, 5999 Stevenson Ave., Alexandria, VA 22304; 800-422-2648; http://www.counseling.org (nonmember, $23.95, member, $19.95).

DE: *Change-Agents; *Counselor-Role; *Social-Action; *Social-Change

DE:Accountability-; Counseling-; Counseling-Objectives; Counseling-Techniques; Cross-Cultural-Studies; Cultural-Awareness; Elementary-Secondary-Education; Public-Policy; Social-Environment

ID: Professionalism-

AB:An increasing number of counselors are becoming agents of social change. Ways in which counselors can enter the arena of social transformation are described in this collection of 18 articles. Following an introduction: (1) "Counselors as Agents of Social Change"—Part I, which focuses on promoting diversity and challenging oppression, contains: (2) "Challenging Intolerance" (I. Grieger; J. G. Ponterotto); (3) "From Multiculturalism to Social Action" (J. A. Lewis; M. S. Arnold); (4) "Challenging Interpersonal Violence" (C. C. Lee; J. L. Brydges); (5) "Gay and Lesbian Activism: A Frontier in Social Advocacy" (B. Barret); (6) "Addressing the Need of At-Risk Youth: Early Prevention and Systemic Intervention" (D. Capuzzi); (7) "Career: Social Action in Behalf of Purpose, Productivity, and Hope" (E. L. Herr; S. G. Niles); (8) "Combating Ageism: The Rights of Older Persons" (J. E. Myers); (9) "Spirituality as a Force for Social Change" (J. G. Miranti; M. T. Burke). Part II, "Social

Action: A Focus on Assessment, Research, and Technology," presents: (10) "Fair Access to Assessment Instruments and the Use of Assessment in Counseling" (N. A. Vacc); (11) "Technology: A Force for Social Action" (J. A. Casey); (12) "The Internet as a Potential Force for Social Change" (J. P. Sampson, Jr.); (13) "Strategies for Social Change Research" (W. E. Sedlacek); (14) "Using the Knowledge Base: Outcome Research and Accountable Social Action" (T. L. Sexton; S. C. Whiston). Part III, "Social Action: A Focus on Professional Issues," features: (15) "Preparing Counselors for Social Action" (B. B. Collison; J. L. Osborne; L. A. Gray; R. M. House; J. Firth; M. Lou); (16) "Interdisciplinary Collaboration for Social Change: Redefining the Counseling Profession" (F. Bemak); (17) "Professional Counseling in a Global Context: Collaboration for International Social Action" (C. C. Lee). The text concludes with "A Summing Up and Call to Action" (C. C. Lee; G. R. Walz). Each chapter contains references. (EMK)

Record 4 of 25 - ERIC

AN: ED413722

AU: Zubal,-Rachael; Shoultz,-Bonnie; Walker,-Pam; Kennedy,-Michael

TI: Materials on Self-Advocacy.

CS: Syracuse Univ., NY. Center on Human Policy.

PY: 1997

DE: *Disabilities-; *Empowerment-; *Personal-Autonomy; *Self-Advocacy; *Self-Determination

DE: Adults-; Decision-Making; Resource-Materials; Social-Support-Groups

AB: This packet of materials focuses on the self-advocacy of individuals with disabilities. Part 1 includes: "Self-Advocacy: Speaking for Yourself" (Michael Kennedy and Patricia Killius), an article written by individuals with disabilities that discusses the importance of people with disabilities making their own decisions and having a say about the services they receive. Strategies for starting a self-advocacy group and the benefits of such a group are described. Part 2, "Resources on Self-Advocacy" (Rachel Zubal, Bonnie Shoultz, and Pam Walker), lists self-advocacy materials that are currently available. Included are resources on choice and self-determination in which the voices of self-advocates were included. Part 3 includes the following articles that all address the need for individuals with disabilities to advocate for themselves and the growth of the self-advocacy movement: "Self-Determination" (Michael Kennedy), "Thoughts about Self-Advocacy" (Michael Kennedy and Bonnie Shoultz), and "More Thoughts about Self-Advocacy: The Movement, The Group and the Individual" (Bonnie Shoultz). (CR)

AN: ED410001

AU: Okun,-Barbara-F.

TI: Understanding Diverse Families: What Practitioners Need To Know.

PY: 1996

ISBN: 1572300566

AV: Guilford Press, 72 Spring Street, New York, NY 10012; phone: 800-365-7006; fax: 212-966-6708; e-mail: staff@guilford.com ($35).

DE: *Adoption-; *Family-Characteristics; *Family-Counseling; *Family-(Sociological-Unit); *Homosexuality-; *Therapy-

DE:Adopted-Children; Adoptive-Parents; Biological-Parents; Child-Development; Counseling-; Counseling-Techniques; Counselor-Attitudes; Counselor-Client-Relationship; Family-Relationship; Family-Structure; Homophobia-; Intermarriage-; Lesbianism-; One-Parent-Family; Racial-Bias; Racial-Identification; Transracial-Adoption

ID: *Interracial-Family

ID: Biracial-Family; Grandparents-as-Parents; Homosexual-Parents; Identity-Formation; Infertility-; Interracial-Children; Reproductive-Technology

AB:Synthesizing current literature with information obtained through interviews of adoptive, gay and lesbian, and multiracial families, this book is designed to help practitioners work with diverse families. An introduction explores the concept of a "normal family" and provides an overview of the book and a description of the interview process. The first chapter, "Diverse Families in Context," provides an overview of diverse families. The next three chapters explore adoptive families: (1) "About Adoption: The Participants in Context" discusses different types of adoptions; (2) "Adapting to Adoption over the Life Span" discusses birth parents, adoptees, and adoptive parents; and (3) "Treatment Issues Pertaining to Adoption" considers infertility, assessment of adoption issues, and treatment and therapist issues. The next three chapters explore homosexual families: (1) "About Homosexuality: The Participants in Context" considers gays and lesbians from a scientific and social historical context, compares heterosexual and homosexual couples and gay and lesbian relationships, and discusses gay and lesbian parenting and its impact on child development; (2) "Homosexuality over the Life Span" talks about lesbian and gay identity formation, the coming-out process, and gay and lesbian couples and families; and (3) "Treatment Issues Pertaining to Homosexuality" discusses therapists' homophobia and other treatment and therapist issues. The next three chapters explore multiracial families: (1) "About Multiraciality: The Participants in Context" gives historical and political background, discusses social science theories about interracial marriage, and talks about race and racism, issues confronting biracial couples and their children, and transracial adoption; (2) "Multiraciality across the Life Span" presents racial identity theories and identity formation of interracial couples and of transracial adoptees and their families; and (3) "Treatment Issues Pertaining to Interracial Couples and Families" discusses therapists' racism and treatment issues with biracial couples, families, and transracial adoptive families. The next chapter, "Emerging Families," discusses single parents by choice, grandparent-led families, and families by artificial reproductive technology. Extensive resources are listed at the end of the book. Contains 408 references. (LPP)

Record 6 of 25 - ERIC

AN: ED399073

TI: Violence and the Family: Report of the American Psychological Association Presidential Task Force on Violence and the Family.

CS: American Psychological Association, Washington, DC.

PY: 1996

AV: American Psychological Association, 750 First Street, NE, Washington, DC 20002-4262.

DE: *Family-Environment; *Family-Violence; *Intervention-; *Victims-of-Crime; *Violence-

DE: Battered-Women; Change-Strategies; Child-Abuse; Cultural-Influences; Elder-Abuse; Family-Problems; Public-Policy; Social-Problems

ID: Resilience-(Personality)

AB: The American Psychological Association (APA) Task Force on Violence and the Family was convened to bring psychological research and clinical experience to bear on the problem of family violence and to make recommendations for solutions. This report of the Task Force highlights the need for a systematic, multi-faceted, multidisciplinary, and multicultural approach to the problem of family violence. Following an executive summary, Part 1 of the report—"Understanding Family Violence and Its Impact"—lays the groundwork for two central assertions: that violence in the family, like all violence, is learned behavior with far-reaching effects; and that family violence is integrally connected to the intensifying levels of violence in society at large. This section contains four chapters: (1) "What Is Family Violence?"; (2) "The Magnitude of Family Violence"; (3) "Risk and Resiliency Factors"; and (4) "The Effects of Family Violence on Society." Part 2 of the report— "Who Are the Victims of Family Violence?"—focuses on what psychology has to say about the people who are direct victims of violence and abuse. This section contains two chapters: (5) "Adult Victims"; and (6) "Child Victims." Part 3 of the report—"Interventions"— focuses on ways to identify, stop, mitigate the consequences of, or prevent family violence. This section contains four chapters: (7) "Interventions for Victims and Survivors"; (8) "Intervening Effectively with Perpetrators"; (9) "Family Violence, Psychology, and the Law"; and (10) "Promoting Violence-Free Families." The final section provides 26 recommendations in 5 broad areas: (1) public policy and intervention; (2) prevention and public education; (3) clinical services; (4) training; and (5) psychological research. An afterword about the Task Force in the context of APA violence-related activities and a list of APA public interest projects on violence from 1984-1996 conclude the report. (EV)

Record 7 of 25 - ERIC

AN: ED397951

TI: Helping Children Affected by Substance Abuse: A Manual for the Head Start Management Team.

CS: Education Development Center, Washington, DC.

PY: 1995

DE:*Alcoholism-; *Drug-Abuse; *High-Risk-Students; *Intervention-; *Program-Improvement; *Substance-Abuse

DE: Agency-Cooperation; Child-Advocacy; Child-Welfare; Childhood-Needs; Children-; Community-Programs; Disadvantaged-Environment; Environmental-Influences; Helping-Relationship; Outreach-Programs; Parent-Participation; Preschool-Education; Social-Services

ID: *Project-Head-Start

ID: Special-Needs-Children

AB: The manual contains technical assistance, information, and suggested strategies for staff who work with children enrolled in Head Start who are affected by substance abuse. The information is intended to bring about change and improvement in the developmental potential of these children. Chapter 1 presents general information on children affected by substance abuse; the impact on their behavior; developmental and educational possibilities; and how the Head Start model lends itself to supporting these children. Chapter 2 highlights effective strategies for improving services, including (1) seven recommended interventions; (2) steps to modify local programs; (3) examples of innovations by local Head Start programs; (4) suggestions for building links among educators, family services, parents, and staff; (5) ways Head Start staff can establish these links; and (6) suggestions for parental and caregiver involvement. Chapter 3 describes techniques to improve program support by facilitating program transitions, training in substance abuse issues, key issues in hiring new staff, strengthening program policies, and finding community partners to support at-risk children. Chapter 4 discusses priorities for resource allocation and tools to use in analyzing the investment needed to implement recommended strategies. Seven exhibits provide checklists and worksheets for management team utilization. (SD)

Record 8 of 25 - ERIC

AN: ED393559

AU: Melton,-Gary-B., ed.

TI: The Individual, the Family, and Social Good: Personal Fulfillment in Times of Change. Nebraska Symposium on Motivation, Volume 42.

PY: 1995

ISBN: 0803282214

AV: University of Nebraska Press, 312 North 14th Street, P.O. Box 880484, Lincoln, NE 68588-0484 (paperback: ISBN-0-8032-8221-4, $20; clothbound: ISBN-0-8032-3185-7).

DE: *Family-Life; *Family-Problems; *Social-Attitudes

DE: Child-Welfare; Communism-; Cultural-Influences; Divorce-; Economic-Factors; Family-Planning; Family-Role; Family-Structure; Family-Violence; Individual-Development; Justice-; Social-Change; Social-Characteristics

ID: Family-Law

AB: The theme of this volume of the Nebraska Symposium on Motivation is the state of contemporary family life and the likelihood of reconciling individual family members' interests with those of the family as a whole. The volume attempts to reflect the dramatic differences that took place within families currently and a generation ago, including changes in family attitudes, family law, everyday attitudes, and motivation. Eight articles are presented in this collection: (1) "Introduction: Personal Satisfaction and the Welfare of Families, Communities, and Society" (Gary B. Melton) provides an overview of changes in various aspects of family life; (2) "Growing Up in a Socially Toxic Environment: Life for Children and Families in 1990s" (James Garbarino) discusses the social context in which children live; (3) "The Deterioration of the Family: A Law and Economics Perspective" (Allen M. Parkman) discusses family formation and the importance of children from the economics and legal points of view; (4) "Community, Family and the Social Good: The Psychological Dynamics of Procedural Justice and Social Identification" (Tom R. Tyler and Peter Degoey) discusses how people develop social motivations, and the legitimacy of authorities; (5) "Social or Individual Orientation? Dilemmas in a Post-Communist World" (Mati Heidmets) discusses social good which attempts to achieve a better understanding of human condition and social transformation; (6) "Social Networks and Family

Violence in Cross-Cultural Perspective" (Jill E. Korbin) discusses family violence and child maltreatment; (7) "Divorce and Custody: The Rights, Needs, and Obligations of Mothers, Fathers and Children" (Eleanor E. Maccoby) discusses parenting obligations, roles and styles; and (8) "Epilogue: Psychology, Law, and the Family" (Ronald Roesch) summarizes the issues discussed in the preceding articles. Each article contains references. (MOK)

Record 9 of 25 - ERIC

AN: ED376376

AU: Newman,-Michael

TI: Defining the Enemy: Adult Education in Social Action.

PY: 1994

ISBN: 0646210521

AV: Stewart Victor Publishing, P.O. Box 51, Paddington, New South Wales 2021, Australia ($34 Australian plus $12 postage and handling).

DE: *Adult-Education; *Adult-Learning; *Educational-Theories; *Learning-Theories; *Social-Action

DE: Activism-; Advocacy-; Environmental-Education; Feminism-; Foreign-Countries; Indigenous-Populations; Labor-Education; Peace-; Social-Change; Unions-; Womens-Education; Womens-Studies

ID: Australia-

AB: This book examines the powerful and motivating kinds of learning that take place when one is in the presence of enemies, such as oppressive employers, bigots, racists, or polluters. It is intended for people interested in education for social action, community development, and political change. The book looks at this kind of learning in aboriginal adult education, trade union training, feminist adult education, peace education, and environmental education. It critically reviews some currently fashionable adult education theories, concluding that a number are simply too nice, too unfocused, too inward looking, or too mechanical to help people who are engaged in social action. It canvasses the ideas of a number of adult educators who have confronted and helped their learners confront exploitation, imposition, and injustice. It proposes some processes that adult educators might use to help people learn how to identify, define, and then deal with their enemies. The argument is developed in clusters of ideas. Links are made using songs, anecdotes, a poem, and quotation from a play. Personal accounts are interwoven with analysis and extensive reference to the literature of adult education. The afterword examines the author's own position in relation to adult education, social action, and violence. Appendixes contain a 140-item bibliography, glossary, and index. (YLB)

Record 19 of 25 - ERIC

AN: ED370446

AU: Graddol,-David, ed.; and-others

TI: Researching Language and Literacy in Social Context.

PY: 1994

ISBN: 1853592218

AV: Multilingual Matters Ltd., Frankfurt Lodge, Clevedon Hall, Victoria Road, Clevedon, Avon, England, BS21 7SJ (paperback: ISBN-1-85359-221-8, $22.95; hardback: ISBN-1-85359-222-6, $69.95).

DE: *Classroom-Communication; *Language-Research; *Literacy-; *Research-Methodology; *Social-Values; *Sociocultural-Patterns

DE: Adults-; Advocacy-; Child-Language; Childrens-Literature; Cultural-Pluralism; Data-Collection; Ethics-; Ethnography-; Indigenous-Populations; Interpersonal-Communication; Literacy-Education; Literary-Criticism; Networks-; Racial-Bias; Reading-Strategies; Research-Design; Researchers-; Role-Perception; Second-Languages; Sex-Differences; Student-Evaluation; Teacher-Student-Relationship; Writing-(Composition)

ID: Turn-Taking

AB: A collection of readings addresses issues in empirical investigation of language and literacy in a social context, and provide models useful to researchers undertaking small-scale studies. They include: "Introducing Ethnography" (Martyn Hammersley); "The Relations between Researcher and Researched: Ethics, Advocacy and Empowerment" (D. Cameron, and others); "Observing and Recording Talk in Educational Settings" (Joan Swann); "Negotiation as a Critical Factor in Learning To Read in a Second Language" (Eve Gregory); "Through Whose Eyes? Exploring Racism through Literature with White Students" (Beverley Naidoo); "'I Treat Them All the Same': Teacher-Pupil Talk in Multi-Ethnic Classrooms" (A. P. Biggs, Viv Edwards); "Reading as a Social Process in a Middle School Classroom" (David Bloome); "Children's Voices: Talk, Knowledge and Identity" (Janet Maybin); "Gender Inequalities in Classroom Talk" (Joan Swann, David Graddol); "Unequal Voices: Gender and Assessment" (Julie Fisher); "No Gap, Lots of Overlap: Turn-Taking Patterns in the Talk of Women Friends" (Jennifer Coates); "Cultural Values in Samish and Australian Children's Literature: A Corpus Linguistic Approach" (Meeri Hellsten); and "Roles, Networks and Values in Everyday Writing" (David Barton, Sarah Padmore). (MSE) (Adjunct ERIC Clearinghouse on

Literacy Education)

Record 10 of 25 - ERIC

AN: ED368148

AU: Bishop,-Kathleen, ed.

TI: Aging, Disabilities, Advocacy and Environmental Design. Annotated Bibliography.

CS: Syracuse Univ., NY. Center on Human Policy.

PY: 1993

DE:*Accessibility-(for-Disabled); *Advocacy-; *Aging-(Individuals); *Developmental-Disabilities; *Physical-Environment

DE: Design-Requirements; Disabilities-; Elementary-Secondary-Education; Environmental-Standards; Older-Adults

AB: This annotated bibliography covers articles, books, and other publications related to aging, advocacy, disabilities, and environmental design. The bibliography brings together these topic areas to demonstrate how environments limit the independent functioning and choice-making opportunities for older adults with developmental disabilities. The bibliography is organized into the following sections: (1) age-related changes (6 listings); (2) aging and self-advocacy for people with developmental disabilities (15 listings); (3) environmental design and aging (12 listings); and (4) further resources (5 catalogs, 3 resource centers, and 17 organizations). (JDD)

Record 11 of 25 - ERIC

AN: ED367521

AU: Farley,-Ronnie, ed.

TI: Women of the Native Struggle. Portraits & Testimony of Native American Women.

PY: 993

ISBN: 0517881136

AV: Crown Publishers, Inc., 201 E. 50th St., New York, NY 10022 ($22).

DE: *Activism-; *Advocacy-; *American-Indians; *Females-

DE: American-Indian-Culture; American-Indian-Education; Child-Rearing; Community-Leaders; Conservation-(Environment); Culture-Conflict; Leadership-; Life-Style; Nonformal-Education; Personal-Narratives

ID: *Spirituality-; *World-Views

ID: Cultural-Preservation; Native-Americans

AB: This book portrays images and views of approximately 45 Native American women in their roles as mothers, grandmothers, tribal elders, teachers, preservers of traditional beliefs and practices, and leaders in the continuing struggle for survival. An introduction by Anna Lee Walter presents an overview of the modern Native American woman. In the section titled "Remembering," the women reflect on daily life in bygone days, experiences in boarding school, life as an Indian in New York City, grandparents' teachings, and community and family connections. "Life Givers" depicts women as the heart of the family and society, the importance of the role of mother, views on feminism and lesbianism, and integration of art with everyday life. "The Light Within" discusses spirituality, sources of inner strength, religious practices, self-esteem, and cross-cultural respect. "The Earth as Our Mother" draws parallels between women's bodies and the Earth and considers the particular responsibilities of women to protect Mother Earth. "The View from the Shore" examines past and present attacks on Native peoples and land, stereotypes and cultural images of American Indians, and threats to the environment from Western mainstream lifestyles. "The Children: Our Future" discusses the women's fears and hopes for the future of their children, instilling spiritual beliefs and cultural pride in children, the importance of culturally relevant education, and alternative culture-based "survival schools." Contains many photographs, brief profiles of the women, and a list of organizations involved in Native American issues. (SV)

Record 13 of 25 - ERIC

AN: ED367445

AU: Webb,-Kelli; and-others

TI: A Guide to Resources on Advocacy: Facts, Strategies, and Information.

CS: Indiana Youth Inst., Indianapolis.

PY: 1992

AV: Indiana Youth Institute, 333 North Alabama Street, Suite 200, Indianapolis, IN 46204 (Order No. RGAD, free; send $2.50 for postage and handling).

DE: *Child-Advocacy; *Community-Information-Services; *Lobbying-; *Mass-Media-Use

DE: Child-Abuse; Child-Welfare; Early-Childhood-Education; Elementary-Secondary-Education; Resource-Materials; Youth-Problems

ID: *Indiana-

AB: This resource guide includes information to help advocates for children be more effective, whether they work at education and research or in direct action with media and legislators. The guide begins with a one-page description of the Indiana Youth Institute (IYI), listing the kinds of youth-related research materials and services it provides. The section titled "Facts" is a three-page listing of various statistics on social problems affecting families, children, and youth in Indiana. The "Strategies" section lists 60 ways to be an advocate; gives advice on how to use mass media; offers pointers on coalition-building; and tells how to work with elected officials and how to find out about federal and state rules for lobbying for nonprofit organizations. The "Information" section lists addresses and phone numbers of statewide child advocacy organizations according to focus (General, Abuse, Diversity, Economics, Education, Employment, Families, Health, Legal and Juvenile Justice, Religion). The section also provides a 22-item bibliography of books on youth advocacy, a list of 7 periodicals, and 1 audiovisual resource about the Indiana State General Assembly. Several excerpts from the books and periodicals are included. The guide ends with an order form for publications sold by IYI, a list of bibliographies available free of charge from IYI, and a feedback survey form for reader reactions on the guide. (ME)

Record 14 of 25 - ERIC

AN: ED359549

AU: Gonzalez,-Roseann-Duenas

TI: Language, Race, and the Politics of Educational Failure: A Case for Advocacy. Concept Paper No. 10.

CS: National Council of Teachers of English, Urbana, IL.

PY: 1993

AV: National Council of Teachers of English, 1111 W. Kenyon Road, Urbana, IL 61801-1096 (Stock No. 38098: $4.95 member, $6.95 nonmembers).

DE: *Academic-Failure; *Child-Advocacy; *Minority-Groups; *Politics-of-Education; *Racial-Factors

DE:American-Indians; Asian-Americans; Educational-Equity-(Finance); Elementary-Secondary-Education; Higher-Education; Hispanic-Americans; Language-Role; Racial-Discrimination

ID: *Educational-Issues

ID: African-Americans; English-Only-Movement; Latinos-; Native-Americans

AB: Painting a picture of the hostile environment in which racial and linguistic minority children live, this paper proposes how educators can become combatants against educational failure that is corrupting the futures and talents of millions of children of color. The paper focuses on the four federally recognized minorities—Latinos, African Americans, Asian Americans, and Native Americans—who make up approximately 95% of the minority population of the United States and who are underrepresented in educational and economic achievement and overrepresented in poverty, joblessness, educational failure and attrition. Sections of the paper discuss: how educators contribute to student failure; attacks on minority culture from the society at large; the "English only" movement; differential treatment established by traditional school funding; identification of the root cause; how educators can become advocates for minority students; and retrieving the dream of the civil rights movement of the 1960s. (Contains 71 references.) (RS)

Record 15 of 25 - ERIC

AN: ED359483

AU: Lucal,-Betsy

TI: Battered Husbands and Battered Wives: Why One Is a Social Problem and the Other Is Not.

PY: 1992

DE: *Battered-Women; *Family-Violence; *Social-Attitudes

DE: Family-Problems; Marital-Instability; Marriage-; Social-Problems; Sociocultural-Patterns; Spouses-

ID: *Battered-Men

AB: A number of factors came together in the 1970s to create a social problem called "battered wives". Then, beginning in 1977, there was an attempt to create a social problem called "battered husbands." So far, such attempts have been unsuccessful. This analysis compares the issue of battered husbands and battered wives to determine why one was successfully constructed as a social problem while the other was not. The development of the two issues is delineated, and then compared. The results of the comparison show that the factors that were present in the construction of battered wives as a social problem—a social movement, professional and mass media attention, and appropriate gender images—were not present for battered husbands. The existence of the feminist movement and the battered women's movement helped establish battered wives as a social problem while gender images supported the notion of women as appropriate and acceptable victims of violence by their husbands. These findings suggest that a climate that supported the existence and maintenance of one of these social problems could not, and has not, supported the institutionalization of the other. (Author/BF)

Record 16 of 25 - ERIC

AN: ED351953

AU: Gill,-Wanda-E.

TI: Perception of Advocacy Issues of Women versus Men.

PY: 1992

DE: *Activism-; *Advocacy-; *Lobbying-; *Political-Issues; *Sex-Differences; *Social-Attitudes

DE: Administrators-; College-Faculty; College-Students; Comparative-Analysis; Females-; Higher-Education; Local-Issues; Males-; Political-Power; Social-Action; Social-Change; Surveys-

ID: Bowie-State-College-MD

AB: This study examined similarities and differences in attitudes between men and women full-time administrators, faculty, staff, and students on various advocacy issues such as harassment, victims' rights, equity, educational funding, and politics. Surveys (N=210) were mailed to faculty, administrators and staff at Bowie State University (Maryland), students in the Student Support Services project, and students enrolled in classes at Ft. Meade, Maryland. Results from the 111 responses received showed that perceptions of advocacy by gender are clear. Generally speaking, it was perceived that national participation by women has produced far greater visibility for women than local or state participation with state level participation seen as the lowest visibility political arena. Women were seen as more likely than men to actively advocate concerning such issues as equity, a harassment free work place, childcare, affordable health care, victims' rights legislation, flex time at work, enforced child support, and increased funding of education. Respondents saw women as less familiar with the political system and lobbying effectiveness as linked to knowledge of the political system. The organizational skills of women were seen as less related to lobbying effectiveness than those of men. Contains 20 references. (GLR)

Record 17 of 25 - ERIC

AN: EJ550312

AU: McWhirter,-Ellen-Hawley

TI: Empowerment, Social Activism, and Counseling.

PY: 1997

SO: Counseling-and-Human-Development; v29 n8 p1-14 Apr 1997

ISSN: 0193-7375

DE: *Advocacy-; *Counseling-Psychology; *Counselor-Role; *Empowerment; *Social-Action

DE: Activism-; Counseling-Techniques; Cultural-Pluralism; Prevention-

ID: Rogers-(Carl)

AB: Defines empowerment and discusses the counseling process in which the goal is empowerment. Describes two underlying assumptions and five core components of counseling for empowerment. Also describes social activism in the context of past and present understanding of the counselor's role. Gives examples of social activism relevant to the counseling profession. (RJM)

Record 18 of 25 - ERIC

AN: EJ442607

AU: Lee,-Courtland-C.; and-others

TI: Indigenous Models of Helping in Nonwestern Countries: Implications for Multicultural Counseling.

PY: 1992

SO: Journal-of-Multicultural-Counseling-and-Development; v20 n1 p3-10 Jan 1992

ISSN: 0883-8534

DE: *Family-Violence; *Helping-Relationship; *Indigenous-Populations; *Mental-Disorders; *Substance-Abuse

DE: Counseling-; Cross-Cultural-Studies; Foreign-Countries; Models-

ID: *Cross-Cultural-Counseling

AB: Examined indigenous models of helping in selected non-Western countries (Barbados, Korea, Nigeria, Pakistan, Singapore, Sudan. and Zambia) to investigate status of psychology, counseling, and related mental health professions in these countries. Findings from mental health professionals in these countries revealed three types of problems for which clients seek help: mental illness, substance abuse, and family violence or pressures. (NB)

Record 19 of 25 - ERIC

AN: ED323715

AU: Harvey,-David-C.

TI: HIV and Mental Health Institutions. AIDS Technical Report, No. 4.

CS: National Association of Protection and Advocacy Systems, Washington, DC.

PY: 1990

AV: National Association of Protection and Advocacy Systems, 200 Eye St., N.E., Suite 150, Washington, DC 2002 ($10.00 each, $40.00 series of 5).

DE:*Acquired-Immune-Deficiency-Syndrome; *Advocacy-; *Mental-Disorders; *Mental-Health; *Program-Evaluation

DE:Adolescents-; Adults-; Agencies-; Case-Studies; Check-Lists; Communicable-Diseases; Confidentiality-; Institutions-; Legal-Responsibility; Policy-Formation; Public-Health; Residential-Programs

AB: This technical report is part of a series on AIDS/HIV (Acquired Immune Deficiency Syndrome/Human Immunodeficiency Virus) and is intended to help link various legal advocacy organizations providing services to persons with mental illness or developmental disabilities. This paper examines AIDS policy issues in mental health institutions. The paper provides a discussion and specific recommendations for policy development for the following areas: (1) education; (2) HIV testing; (3) confidentiality; (4) duty to protect; (5) liability; and (6) access to services. Also included is a summary of interviews with four administrators at Washington D.C. institutions which demonstrate the daily issues confronting institutions. Includes 15 references. (DB)

Record 20 of 25 - ERIC

AN: ED294077

TI: Where to Turn for Help for Older Persons: A Guide for Action on Behalf of An Older Person.

CS: Administration on Aging (DHHS), Washington, DC.

PY: 987

AV: Superintendent of Documents, U.S. Government Printing Office, Washington, DC 20402.

DE: *Advocacy-; *Helping-Relationship; *Human-Services; *Older-Adults

DE: Community-Services; Financial-Problems; Health-Services; Housing-; Legal-Problems

AB: This guide was written to help persons find help when they are faced with an urgent situation regarding an elderly family member, friend, or neighbor. It provides guidance as to where to find help in the community where the older person lives. The first section of the guide contains the most frequently asked questions in significant areas of life, giving each question a page and item number to help readers locate information in the guide. A financial section describes the Older Americans Act, Social Security, Supplemental Security Income, Medicare, Medicaid, other public supported programs, private resources, home equity conversion, property tax exemptions, tax benefits, and senior citizen benefits. A health section looks at medical, psychiatric, hospital, and emergency services; hospice programs; and nursing home care. The community services section discusses information and referral, emergencies, transportation, in-home care, chore services, home improvement, medical equipment, nutrition, respite care, adult day care, counseling, support groups, reassurance, and social activities. Legal issues addressed include power of attorney, durable power of attorney, guardianship, wills, living wills, and other issues. The section on shelter reviews several housing options for older adults. The final section of the guide lists names and telephone numbers for State Agencies on Aging for the 50 states, the District of Columbia, Samoa, Guam, Puerto Rico, Trust Territory of the Pacific Islands, and the Virgin Islands. (NB)

Record 21 of 25 - ERIC

AN: ED224747

TI: Youth Participation in Youth Advocacy: A Practical Guide for Developing Programs.

CS: National Commission on Resources for Youth, Inc., Boston, MA.

PY: 1982

AV: National Commission on Resources for Youth, Inc., 605 Commonwealth Ave., Boston, MA 02215 ($5.00).

DE: *Advocacy-; *Community-Programs; *Models-; *Program-Development; *Youth-Programs

DE: Adolescents-; Case-Studies; Guidelines-; Justice-; Participative-Decision-Making; Program-Descriptions; Program-Implementation; Secondary-Education; Social-Action; Social-Systems; Young-Adults

AB: Guidelines and case studies of model programs are intended as resource materials to aid 22 organizations funded by the Office of Juvenile Justice and Delinquency Prevention to encourage meaningful youth participation in policy decisions which affect youth, primarily in the juvenile justice, educational, and social systems. The first of three major parts briefly discusses why youth participation is essential, what youth gain from participation, and the key elements of youth participation. The second part provides practical guidelines for program implementation on organizational commitment, qualities of youth organizers, recruitment, incentives, getting youth interested in advocacy, developing commitment, training, skills, and opportunities for learning. The third part, comprising over half of the publication, describes a variety of advocacy activities that young people have handled successfully in actual projects developed to respond to local needs using local resources. They publish newspapers; produce handbooks, comic books, and guides; produce radio shows; and negotiate with public officials, and develop legislation. (RM)

Record 22 of 25 - ERIC

AN: EJ427140

TI: Recommendations for the 21st Century.

PY: 1991

SO: Child-Abuse-and-Neglect:-The-International-Journal; v15 suppl 1 p39-50 1991

ISSN: 0145-2134

DE:*Change-Strategies; *Child-Abuse; *Child-Advocacy; *Child-Welfare; *Law-Enforcement

DE: Child-Neglect; Community-Programs; Conferences-; Delivery-Systems; Discussion-Groups; Futures-(of-Society); Health-Services; Legislation-; Medical-Services; Mental-Health; Prevention-; Sexual-Abuse; Social-Work

AB: Group discussions on physical, sexual, and emotional child abuse and neglect, which took place at the "Child Protection for the 21st Century Conference," are summarized. The discussions noted practices that should be preserved and those requiring change in law/law enforcement, mental health, medicine/nursing, social work, and prevention and community advocacy. (JDD)

Record 23 of 25 - ERIC

AN: EJ414645

AU: Agresti,-Albert-A.

TI: AIDS Education: Professional Ethics, Social Advocacy, and Religious Values.

PY: 1990

SO: Counseling-and-Values; v34 n3 p217-19 Apr 1990

ISSN: 0160-7960

DE: *Acquired-Immune-Deficiency-Syndrome; *Counseling-Services; *Ethics; *Health-Education; *Religious-Factors; *Social-Responsibility

DE: Advocacy-; Professional-Personnel; Social-Values

ID: Self-Monitoring

AB: Encourages Acquired Immune Deficiency Syndrome education efforts to attend to religious pluralism in society and to illustrate the self-monitoring that is identified with professional activity. Claims this monitoring will help avoid possible compromise of the public's trust and confidence in counselors' work. (Author/ABL)

Record 24 of 25 - ERIC

AN: EJ411829

AU: Kelker,-Katharin-A.

TI: School Services for Drug-Addicted Children: What Parents Need to Know.

PY: 1990

SO: Preventing-School-Failure; v34 n3 p22-24 Spr 1990

DE: *Behavior-Problems; *Child-Advocacy; *Educational-Legislation; *Parent-Participation; *Substance-Abuse

DE:Advocacy-; Alcohol-Abuse; Drug-Abuse; Elementary-Secondary-Education; Individualized-Education-Programs; Parent-School-Relationship; Student-Placement

ID: *Education-for-All-Handicapped-Children-Act; *Rehabilitation-Act-1973-(Section-504)

AB: This article discusses applications of education legislation for drug-addicted children, including the Education for All Handicapped Children Act and Sec. 504 of the Rehabilitation Act of 1973, which recognizes smoking and drug addiction as handicapping conditions. Suggested guidelines for parents seeking school support services under these laws are offered. (PB)

Record 25 of 25 - ERIC

AN: EJ411390

AU: Woodside,-Marianne-R.; Legg,-Bobbie-H.

TI: Patient Advocacy: A Mental Health Perspective.

PY: 1990

SO: Journal-of-Mental-Health-Counseling; v12 n1 p38-50 Jan 1990

DE: *Advocacy-; *Institutionalized-Persons; *Mental-Disorders

DE: Counselor-Client-Relationship; Mental-Health; Patients-

AB: Discusses the Protection and Advocacy for Mentally Ill Individuals Act of 1986. Describes recent mental health reform history. Defines patient advocates' role and responsibilities. Presents illustrations of types of cases encountered by patient advocate. Explores implications of this role for the mental health counselor. (Author/CM)

About ERIC and ERIC/CASS

ERIC/CASS (originally ERIC/CAPS) was one of the original Clearinghouses which formed the Educational Resources Information Center (ERIC) in 1966. ERIC has since grown to be the world's largest educational data base with nearly one million entrees.

The ERIC system has as its mission to improve American education by increasing and facilitating the use of educational research and information on practice in the activities of learning, teaching, educational decision-making, and research, wherever and whenever these activities take place.

ERIC is made up of sixteen separate Clearinghouses, each of which has a specific focus. The ERIC Counseling & Student Services Clearinghouse (ERIC/CASS) has its major foci serving the needs and interests of care givers and helping specialists such as counselors, therapists, career specialists, etc., at all ages and educational levels and in all settings—school, college, government, business and private practice.

Our basic goal has been to improve decision making through increased access to information. More importantly, we strive through the many resources and services we offer, to empower our users to more fully realize their goals and — yes—their dreams as well!

NETWORK WITH ERIC/CASS!

On a regular basis ERIC/CASS disseminates information about important topics to members of special interest and professional focus networks. Among the items distributed are newsletters, announcements of new products and resources, ERIC Digests, new releases, workshop and conference information, and updates on new developments in ERIC and information technology. If you are interested in becoming an ERIC/CASS Networker, please complete this form.

Name: _____

Preferred Title: ☐ Mr. ☐ Mrs. ☐ Ms. ☐ Dr.

Address: _____

_____

City: _____ State: _____ Zip: _____

Phone Numbers:

Home: _____ Office: _____

FAX: _____

Internet Address : _____

Position: Level/Setting:
_Counselor/Therapist   _ Elementary School   _ Community Agency
_School Psychologist   _ Middle/Junior High School _ Government Agency
_Social Worker   _ High School   _ Professional
_Counselor Educator   _ K-12/District Office   Association
_School Psych. Educator _ Intermediate School Dist. _ Private Practice
_Social Work Educator   _ Junior/Community College   _ Other
_Administrator   _ College/University
_Student
_Other

Major Interests:

1. _____   2. _____   3. _____

Mail To:
ERIC/CASS NETWORKER
201 Ferguson Building
University of North Carolina at Greensboro
PO Box 26171
Greensboro, NC 27402-6171
FAX (336) 334-4116

ERIC...FOR ALL YOUR INFORMATION NEEDS!

ERIC

ERIC (Educational Resources Information Center) is a national information system that provides ready access to an extensive body of education-related literature. Through its 16 subject-specific clearinghouses and four support components, ERIC provides a variety of services and products including acquiring and indexing documents and journal articles, producing publications, responding to requests, and distributing microfilmed materials to libraries nationwide. In addition, ERIC maintains a database of over 800,000 citations to documents and journal articles.

ERIC/CASS

The ERIC Counseling and Student Services Clearinghouse (ERIC/CASS) was one of the original clearinghouses established in 1966. Its scope area includes school counseling, school social work, school psychology, mental health counseling, marriage and family counseling, career counseling, and student development.

Topics covered by ERIC/CASS include the training, supervision, and continuing professional development of counseling, college student services and development professionals, as well as adult counseling and mental health professionals. Other up-to-date and relevant topics include:

(a) counseling theories, research methods, and practices;
(b) the roles of counselors, social workers, and psychologists in all educational settings at all educational levels;
(c) career planning and development;
(d) self-esteem and self-efficacy;
(e) marriage and family counseling; and
(f) counseling services to special populations such as substance abusers, pregnant teenagers, students at risk and public offenders.

ERIC/CASS exists to serve anyone who has a need to access information related to counseling and student services with quick and friendly assistance to retrieve information related to counseling and human services. Print indexes (RIE and CIJE), on-line searches, and ERIC on CD-ROM can be helpful in locating what is needed.

How To Access Information

The most convenient method of gaining access to the information is to contact a local public, college, or university library that provides ERIC database search services. The customer service staff at **1-800-LET-ERIC (538-3742)** can provide information about the location in your area.

Customers can also access ERIC Clearinghouses or the central ERIC facility via the Internet at **http://www.accesseric.org:81/** You may conduct your own search of the ERIC database on the Internet by visiting the ERIC Document Reproduction Service at: **http:// edrs.com/**.Complete instructions and tips for targeting your search are provided.

You can send an e-mail question and receive a return e-mail usually within 48 hours. The reply will contain a mini-search of the ERIC d atabase with references to ERIC documents and journal articles as well as suggestions for other sources of information relevant to your question. Send an e-mail to: **askeric@ askeric.org** or search the website at: **http:askeric.org**.

Contact Us Directly

Should these options be unavailable to you, contact ERIC/ CASS directly for your information needs. We are able to electronically search and retrieve information based upon descriptors and key words as well as bibliographic information such as author, publication date, etc. You may request a search via a letter or fax indicating subjects, topics, key words or phrases, etc., that you wish to focus upon. You may also contact us by telephone **(800/414-9769)** or e-mail **(ericcass@uncg.edu)** so that we may discuss your needs and assist you in focusing your search in order to provide results as specific as possible.

More Resources From ERIC/CASS

ERIC/CASS is an active user of electronic communication. The CASS website features an array of targeted virtual libraries that offer users access to an unparalleled abundance of resources on priority educational topics including materials from the U.S. Department of Education and the National Library of Education. These on-line functioning libraries provide a wealth of free, fulltext resources which can be downloaded and instantly put to use.

Access the user-friendly ERIC/CASS virtual libraries website at:

http://www.uncg.edu/edu/ericcass/libhome.htm

INTERNATIONAL CAREER DEVELOPMENT LIBRARY

Where to Go When You Want to Know...developed and managed by NOICC & ERIC/CASS.

The *ICDL* is a Virtual Library available to anyone with an Internet connection. It features a wide range of books and resources covering all aspects of career development for all age levels and for practitioners, researchers and educators, as well as students and parents. With the ongoing assistance of professional organizations and Department of Education components such as NLE and ERIC, it has exceptionally comprehensive and intensive coverage. Some of its present features as well as ones which will be added in the future are listed below. Like any new major development, it has to be seen and experienced to appreciate it, so check it out now!

SPECIAL FEATURES

- Fulltext database of career development materials
- Customized search engine
- Interactive discussions of compelling career issues
- Original papers by experts in the field posted on-line
- An electronic library card with career information filtering properties
- Comprehensive list of links to quality career websites around the world
- Information and updates on related training registries
- Networking with cvolleagues around the world

Access the International Career Development Library at:
http://icdl.uncg.edu/

ERIC Publications: In Print And On-line

ERIC/CASS publications provide resources which respond to your needs. Written by expert researchers, scholars, and practitioners, they range from two-page information digests to in-depth monographs and books. ERIC/CASS publications are well-known for their intensive and up-to-date analyses of high priority topics. We also offer selected publications from other professional associations and commercial sources.

For information on ERIC/CASS publications, call for a catalog **(800/414-9769)** or you may order from our on-line catalog at: **http://www.uncg.edu/edu/ericcass**.

The ERIC/CASS Newsletter

ERIC/CASS regularly announces new publications and digests, important developments in OERI and the Department of Education, and the availability of specialized training through workshops, conferences, and conventions. The CASS newsletter is the usual way of updating members of the CASS network as to available resources and future developments. Call the CASS 800 number and request to join the network.

The ERIC/CASS Virtual Libraries

Be sure to visit the ERIC Counseling and Student Services Online Virtual Libraries. Each Virtual Library is designed to provide users with online access to an extensive array of full-text documents on a current HOT topic of critical concern.

The libraries include:
- CAREER DEVELOPMENT
- CULTURAL DIVERSITY
- SCHOOL VIOLENCE
- STUDENT ACHIEVEMENT
- SUBSTANCE ABUSE
- CONFLICT RESOLUTION
- DEPRESSION AND SUICIDE
- BULLYING IN SCHOOLS
- YOUTH GANGS
- JUVENILE BOOT CAMPS

Access the ERIC counseling and student services homepage at: **http://www.uncg.edu/edu/ericcass**

ERIC Clearinghouse on Counseling & Student Services
School of Education • 201 Ferguson Building
The University of North Carolina at Greensboro
PO Box 26171 • Greensboro, NC 27402-6171
800-414-9769 • e-mail: ericcass@uncg.edu